GIVING AND RECEIVING COUNSEL

Mutual Admonition and Life Together in the Hutterite Tradition

JESSE D. HOFER

Cover Image: Lyceum Library, Department of Historical Book Collections, Central Library of the Slovak Academy of Sciences (*Lyceálna knižnica, Kabinet historických knižných fondov, Ústredná knižnica Slovenskej akadémie vied*), MS vol. 388 (*Rkp. zv. 388*), fol. 48v.

The artistic representation of Jacob D. Maendel used for the Jacob D. Maendel Lectures logo was designed by Brendan Maendel.

All scripture quotations, unless otherwise noted, are from the New Revised Standard Version Updated Edition (NRSVue), © 2021 National Council of Churches of Christ in the United States of America. Used by permission. All rights reserved worldwide.

ISSN 2562-7481

ISBN 978-1-998141-16-6

Library and Archives Canada Cataloguing in Publication
Title: Giving and receiving counsel : mutual admonition and life together in the Hutterite tradition / Jesse Hofer.
Names: Hofer, Jesse, author. | Hutterian Brethren Book Centre, publisher.
Description: Series statement: The 2025 Jacob D. Maendel lectures, 2562-7481
Identifiers: Canadiana 2025024604X | ISBN 9781998141166 (softcover)
Subjects: LCSH: Hutterian Brethren.
Classification: LCC BX8129.H8 H52 2025 | DDC 289.7/3—dc23

Box 40 • MacGregor, MB • R0H 0R0
p. 204-272-5132 • f. 204-252-2381 • e. orders@hbbookcentre.com

The 2025
Jacob D. Maendel Lectures
were presented at
Trinity United Church, Portage la Prairie, MB
on May 31, 2025.

TABLE OF CONTENTS

INTRODUCTION

There is a growing sense that the Hutterite communities of today stand at something of an impasse. On the one hand lies the enduring impulse to preserve tradition, to hold fast to the structures, values, and practices that have long defined communal life. On the other, there is a genuine desire—especially among the younger generation—for renewal, innovation, and deeper engagement with scripture and discipleship within the Hutterite context. This tension is not new, but it is perhaps more acutely felt now, as communities navigate the challenges and opportunities of life in the twenty-first century.[1]

This tension surfaces a host of difficult and often controversial questions that strike at the heart of Hutterite identity and practice. What is the role of leadership, and where does true authority reside: in tradition, in scripture, in the brotherhood (i.e., the body of baptized members who share in the full responsibilities of communal life)—or a combination of these and other factors? How should communities understand and engage with their historical textual heritage, in particular, the collection of historical homilies? The ongoing language debate—whether to maintain the archaic German of the religious texts or shift to English—touches on questions of identity and accessibility; what about the Hutterisch dialect? At the same time, the influence of North American evangelical fundamentalism have introduced new theological emphases and individualist tendencies that sometimes sit uneasily with com-

---

1   For a historical survey of this tension, see Astrid von Schlachta, *"Holding Fast to What Is Good?" Tradition and Renewal in Hutterite History* (MacGregor: Hutterian Brethren Book Centre, 2022).

munal traditions. These are not merely abstract concerns; they are questions that shape daily life, worship, and the Hutterite future.

To engage these questions faithfully requires both courage and care—an openness to dialogue, and a willingness to be challenged by one another and by scripture. It is not enough to preserve the past; we must also seek to understand to what God is calling us in the here and now.

This publication of the 2025 Jacob D. Maendel Lectures is offered in the hope that it may serve as a resource for thoughtful and faithful reflection on what it means to live as Hutterites in Christian community today. It is intended not as a prescriptive text, but as a kind of provocation—fodder for discussion and discernment. In particular, it seeks to enrich ongoing conversations about the nature of communal life, the practice of giving and receiving counsel, and the spiritual formation of youth and adults alike.

Each lecture is accompanied by a set of discussion questions. These are designed to support further reflection in each reader's unique context, and may be especially useful in settings such as community book clubs, Sunday school classes, or more informal group discussions. Whether used in intergenerational gatherings or among peer groups, these questions are meant to invite dialogue, encourage storytelling, and cultivate a shared vocabulary for thinking about life together in Christ.

Included as an appendix is Jesse Hofer's previously published work on cultivating a culture of dialogue within Hutterite communities.[2] Though there is minor overlap with the new material presented here, the essay has been reproduced without alteration because it complements the lectures and may be easier for some readers to engage with here than in the more academic volume where it first appeared.

I want to express thanks to Jesse for his thoughtful contribution to this lecture series. His work on the practice of giving and receiving

---

2   Jesse D. Hofer, "Building Capacity for Communal Conversation: Gemeindeordnungen and Discernment in the Hutterite World," in *Navigating Tradition and Innovation: Essays Commemorating the Permanent Settlement of Hutterites in Manitoba*, ed. Kenny Wollmann (MacGregor, MB: Hutterian Brethren Book Centre, 2024), 321–45.

counsel within the Hutterite tradition draws deeply from historical sources, personal experience, and biblical conviction. It is my hope that his reflections will continue to shape the ways in which communities nurture faith, accountability, and mutual care for years to come.

Kenny Wollmann
July 2025

How very good and pleasant it is
    when kindred live together in unity!

It is like the precious oil on the head,
    running down upon the beard,
on the beard of Aaron,
    running down over the collar of his robes.

It is like the dew of Hermon,
    which falls on the mountains of Zion.
For there the Lord ordained his blessing,
    life forevermore.

PSALM 133[*]

---

[*] For its earliest audience, this psalm expressed dreams of national unity through the image of a priestly anointing. For believers today, it reinforces the New Testament idea that all believers are equipped with God's Spirit and are called to serve the priestly role of mediating God's blessings to the world.

LECTURE ONE
Early Hutterite Visions of Life Together

In 1560, a little more than thirty years after the first communities were established in Moravia, Hutterite minister and missioner Claus Felbinger, also known as Claus Schlosser after his occupation as a locksmith, was captured near Landshut in Bavaria (southern Germany today). Felbinger had been elected servant of the Word in 1558, and two years later, he and brother Hans Leutner were sent on a mission to Bavaria, where they were arrested a week before Easter 1560.

The brothers were imprisoned, and over the following ten weeks they were tortured and interrogated in an attempt to force them to recant, before being executed. During this time, Felbinger wrote a modest confession of about twenty pages. It was a popular resource for Hutterite missioners because of its concise and rich descriptions of core Hutterite beliefs and practices.

Felbinger's text contains many of the standard topics found in sixteenth-century confessions, based on questions put to him: a critique of infant baptism and the sacramental understanding of the Lord's Supper, an explanation of why oath swearing is problematic, an urgent appeal to freedom in matters of faith, and so on. Today, I'd like to focus on the parts of Felbinger's confession that speak to the question of life together in Christian community.

It is worth noting at the outset that Felbinger's *Rechenschaft* (confession of faith) doesn't include an explicit defence of *Güter-gemeinschaft* (community-of-goods), but it does include a compelling description of *Geistes-gemeinschaft*, the animating spirit behind the sharing of wealth.[1] Instead of defending economic communalism, Felbinger highlights the fact that Christian community involves the sharing of our whole lives—our unique gifts, our precious time, our wise counsel, our living bodies, and yes, our money, too.

One of the questions put to Felbinger by his interlocutors was: "Why do you not stay here [in Bavaria]? Is it not possible to live a good life here and be saved? Or is salvation confined to Moravia?"[2] Felbinger responded by saying that salvation is definitely not limited to a particular place, but persecution had prevented the Hutterites from living in other places. Furthermore, their frank speech against wickedness and injustice had resulted in alienation and public anger against them.

Felbinger goes on to explain why it is essential that believers share their lives with each other. He writes,

> Whoever fears God and does what is right is pleasing to God, but the true children of God eagerly draw together and do not remain apart from each other, so they can encourage one another. For a devout person is never happier than when they are in the company of their brothers and sisters, where they can share love and goodness, with devotion and honour, for it is the character of divine love to be in the neighbour's debt, to serve wholeheartedly, and to do so with joy.[3]

There is a lot in this passage that gets at the heart of what it means to live in Christian community. First, Felbinger recognizes that there is an irreducibly social or relational element to the Christian faith. When a person comes to faith, they are naturally drawn to gather with other believers in order to experience the new life,

---

1   Felbinger does quote Acts 4:32-35, but his overall arguments focus on the spiritual motivations of communalism.

2   "*Abschrüfft des gelaubens,*" Lyceum Library, Department of Historical Book Collections, Central Library of the Slovak Academy of Sciences (*Lyceálna knižnica, Kabinet historických knižných fondov, Ústredná knižnica Slovenskej akadémie vied*), MS vol. 388 (*Rkp. zv. 388*), fol. 75r (translated by the author). See also Claus Felbinger, "Claus Felbinger's Confession of 1560," trans. Robert Friedmann, *Mennonite Quarterly Review* 29 (April 1955): 156.

3   "*Abschrüfft des gelaubens,*" 76r; "Claus Felbinger's Confession," 156.

the new way of being human that God has opened up for them through the life, teaching, and spirit of Jesus. Brothers and sisters are drawn to live and work together because they can be a source of comfort and encouragement for each other, and they can serve each other in love, with all their strength. This service, and being with others in love, draws strength and inspiration from God's love, which is generous, sacrificial, self-emptying, and concerned for the other. Finally, when done in this spirit, it is a great joy.

Felbinger's vision of Christian community is based on his under-standing of the nature of the church: The church is the body of Christ, whose members are knit together by the love of God. Each member of Christ's body has a valuable gift to share to ensure the body's growth, its repair, and its overall health and integrity. In Felbinger's words, echoing 1 Peter 4:10–11:

> Each devout heart refreshes the other with the gift
> it has received from God, for the building up of
> the body of Christ, his holy fellowship, which in-
> cludes all believing and faithful hearts who have
> been bound together by God's love.[4]

This insight is fundamental for appreciating the gift and responsib-ility of mutual admonition, or of giving and receiving counsel, in a Christian community. At its essence, the Christian life is a new way of relating to others and a new way of being with others, and thus, in the fellowship of the faithful, each member is expected to bring their gifts to share at the common table—and these gifts are to be welcomed. The role of leadership is to articulate a clear vision of where the community is heading and to enable its members to see this vision and to actively participate in pursuing it. This includes helping people recognize and cultivate their gifts, and encouraging them to share those gifts with the wider community.

A Priesthood of All Believers

Early Anabaptists resonated with the priesthood-of-all-believers doctrine popularized by Martin Luther. This teaching challenged and collapsed the two-tier hierarchy between the ordained clergy

---

4   *"Abschrüfft des gelaubens,"* 77v; "Claus Felbinger's Confession," 156.

and the non-ordained laity, and emphasized that every member is called to participate in the life of the church community. It was assumed that each member had been given the Spirit of God to exercise these gifts in a spirit of humility and generosity, and thus had something valuable to contribute.

The idea that every believer is called to be a priest and to contribute to the body is communicated clearly in a hymn called, "*Der Jünger Christi Zeichen ist*," found in the so-called *Lutherisches Gesangbuch*:

> 11. Even if we are not all pastors
> love still binds us together
> to struggle for the neighbour's soul
> the preaching office is not neglected
> but is made more fruitful
> when we help in this way.

> 12. Every Christian is a priest
> inspired by the Holy Spirit
> to be mindful of their neighbour's salvation;
> those who share Jesus' mindset
> and love God's honour and kingdom
> cannot dismiss this teaching.[5]

Felbinger concludes his discussion of why living in a community of believers is important by emphasizing that the gathered community of faith living in this loving way has the important function of teaching or discipling its members through the compelling witness of faithful disciples: "There one sees holy witnesses, good examples in word and deed, that inspire others to discipleship."[6] God's salvation is not only found in Moravia, says Felbinger; wherever it is found, it has something to do with God's people living in a radically new way that includes mutual accountability and sharing of gifts.

---

5 "*Der Jünger Christi Zeichen ist: wenn aus dem Herzen Liebe fliesst* [The mark of a disciple of Christ is this: when love flows from the heart]," in *Gesangbuch: Eine Sammlung geistlicher Lieder zur Allgemeinen Erbauung und zum Lohe Gottes*, Elkhart: Mennonite Publishing Company, 1918), 331, no. 264 (translated by the author). In the Hutterite tradition, this hymnal is colloquially referred to as the "*Lutherisches Gesangbuch*," likely because of the presence of many Lutheran chorale texts.

6 "*Abschrüfft des gelaubens*," 77v; "Claus Felbinger's Confession," 156.

To summarize, Felbinger highlights three reasons why living among brothers and sisters in community is indispensable:

1. We can express God's love by comforting and encouraging each other to be faithful.

2. Empowered and renewed by God's Spirit, we can share our gifts with each other to build up the body of Christ.

3. We can be "holy examples" or witnesses that attract others—whether it be our youth, other members, or outsiders—to participate in the life God has made possible through Christ.

Everything Felbinger has said so far points to a community whose members are drawn together by their common love of God and their commitment to following Jesus, who will actively give counsel to and receive counsel from each other. It is this commitment I want to explore further, with questions such as:

* What does it mean to be the people of God?

* Why are we called to live this way? What biblical and theological teachings support this vision?

* What shape should our life together have so all gifts are valued, nurtured, and shared?

* What role does "giving and receiving counsel" play in our communities today, and how might we enrich and extend our understandings and practices around giving and receiving counsel?

The Witness of Hans Schmied

Before exploring these questions, I want to share some words from another sixteenth-century Hutterite witness: Hans Schmied.

Hans Schmied joined the Hutterites in 1581. In 1590, toward the end of the Golden Years, he was captured and imprisoned in Württemberg, his home territory. He spent time in several different prisons, endured torture, and was eventually released.

When Schmied was accused by his interrogators of being a disgrace to his father and violating the fourth commandment by leaving his parents and joining the Hutterites, he explained, "I could not be faithful [*fromm*] in the world. I tried many times, but it did not last half an hour."[7] In other words, there was something about the way of being together among the Hutterian Brethren that helped him grow as a disciple and remain faithful.

In the conclusion to his account of his missionary travels and time in prison, Schmied expresses his deep gratitude for being able to live among believers, where "the Lord's word, the comfort of souls" is made available in a way that was not accessible to him before.

> I thank God that he kept me faithful and led me again to the children of God. … For the pleasant living together of the devout or the children of God is the most precious jewel, which I treasure in my heart and cannot be compared to anything on earth.…
>
> How good it is to be with the devout, where one can receive the Lord's word, the comfort of the soul: Where the zealous can find instruction, the troubled can find good counsel, the sick can find a physician, the weak a place of rest and shelter; where the righteous can receive justice, and to the unrighteous his unrighteousness can be pointed out. The hungry can find bread, the thirsty receive drink. How good it is if one can have the bright light of day and need not be shut up in darkness![8]

Like Felbinger, Schmied recognizes the gift of a community where he can be held accountable, where he can "find instruction… and good counsel" where each member can contribute and find what they need to grow and be faithful. Is the vision articulated by these two sixteenth-century brothers shared by Hutterites today? Is the kind of support and care described by them commonly available in

---

7   *"Eine kurze Beschreibung von unserm lieben Bruder Hans Schmied* [A brief Account of our dear brother Hans Schmied]," *Die Hutterischen Episteln*, vol. 4 (Elie: James Valley Book Centre, 1991), 130. For the English version, "Hans Schmied's Experiences in Württemberg," see page 552.

8   *"Eine kurze Beschreibung,"* 146–147; "Hans Schmied's Experiences in Württemberg," 559.

our communities? Do we consider this aspect of our life together as a treasure to be cultivated and protected?

You Are Too Ambitious!

What is this vision of Christian community described by Claus Felbinger and Hans Schmied based on? What gave them the audacity to think this kind of life was possible?

The Landshut authorities who interrogated Felbinger accused him of being unrealistic, overly ambitious, and naïve about the human condition. After all, humans are sinful, and will continue to be this way even if they are part of a Christian congregation. Felbinger critiques this notion of "cheap grace" by emphasizing that true repentance and the new birth will necessarily translate to a transformed life. He writes,

> They think we aim far too high; that Christ has already sufficiently paid for our sins; that we only need to believe this, recognize that we are sinners, and God will be gracious and merciful. They make no mention of the new birth, without which no one can be saved, and they are silent about authentic repentance, which means to sin no more, to begin a new life, and not to be conformed to the world.[9]

Here we see the Anabaptist-Hutterite emphasis on the experience of repentance and the new birth, "a new and holy life in God," which would give rise to a church of disciplined, faithful members. In contrast to the notion of Christendom—that essentially everyone in the Holy Roman Empire was a Christian, and it was therefore impossible to discern who was a sincere believer—the Anabaptists insisted that true faith would lead to a radical change in one's life, allegiance and conduct. Only those willing to make a commitment to "walk in newness of life,"[10] following Jesus as Lord in word and deed, would receive baptism into the body. Baptism into the body meant, among other things, accepting mutual admonition and correction, including church discipline and the

9   *"Abschrüfft des gelaubens,"* 62v; "Claus Felbinger's Confession," 150.
10   Rom 6:4.

ban. The Lord's Supper, meanwhile, was understood as a meal of remembrance, which included a testing of one's ongoing commitment to the body of Christ.[11] Am I, too, prepared to die rather than betray my brothers and sisters to the enemy, even under torture? This was a very real possibility in the sixteenth-century context in which Felbinger was writing.

It is not surprising that Felbinger's interrogators accused him of being too optimistic about human nature. After all, this is a very high ideal to aim for, one that, apart from the enlivening spirit of Christ, is impossible to achieve. And of course, Hutterites often failed to realize this ideal; one only needs to read the *Ordnungen* from that period to see that they didn't always live up to it. Yet Felbinger insists that the life he is describing is possible, precisely because of the work God has done in his people through Jesus and continues to do through his Spirit. He grounds his confidence and his vision of community in his personal experience of the living God moving to create new life. Felbinger writes,

> I will not hold back from speaking about what is right in God's eyes, especially what I have seen and heard and experienced in my heart through the renewal of the Holy Spirit: namely, of the resurrection of Jesus Christ, who has created new life in those of us who believe and honour his name, and have committed and submitted ourselves to him completely.[12]

Further, Felbinger points out that it is Jesus' victory over Satan that gives him the confidence to believe that it is possible to leave behind a sinful life and participate in a community that gives and receives counsel. To think otherwise would be to deny God's power and, especially, the gift of Jesus' life, death, and resurrection.

> For they do not think it is possible to serve God in true obedience, without sin. If it were not possible to abandon the godless and sinful life, which is the work of the devil, then Satan would be stronger

---

11   C. Arnold Snyder, *Following in the Footsteps of Christ: The Anabaptist Tradition* (Maryknoll: Orbis Books, 2004), 101.

12   *"Abschrüfft des gelaubens,"* 58v; "Claus Felbinger's Confession," 148.

than God. God forbid! Christ was sent into this world by the Father to take away the power of the devil, the old serpent, to crush his head, to destroy his works and banish sin, that is, from all who gladly let their sins be taken away.[13]

To summarize, Felbinger can be confident about the possibility of following Jesus in Christian community because he has experienced God's liberating power. It bears repeating: A community of faith where members share their gifts to build up the body is only possible by the power of God. Through his life, death, and resurrection, God in Christ has defeated Satan and his grip on us by inviting us into a new shared life of being with others in a spirit of radical truthfulness, tenderness, vulnerability, and trust. Held by a community of care, where giving and receiving counsel in the spirit of Jesus is practised, Claus Felbinger and Hans Schmied can boldly proclaim: We live *this* way because we need each other to remain faithfully aligned with the way of Jesus, and we live this way to be a witness to the watching world.

Giving and Receiving Counsel: Defining Terms

One of the essential gifts and challenges for those seeking to live a life in an intentional faith community is mutual admonition. I want to consider the terminology we use around this practice as a way to think about the expectations we have for it.

Based on Matthew 18:15–17, early Anabaptists understood mutual admonition and church discipline, also known as the "rule of Christ," as an essential mark of the true church.[14] Because of their commitment to a disciplined church, they resorted to the ban to ensure accountability and growth in holiness in their congregations. Over the years, Anabaptists have rightfully been criticized for how they have sometimes applied the ban in a hurtful and manipulative fashion. Nevertheless, the insight behind this practice—that believers need to hold each other accountable—is indispensable for authentic Christian community.

---

13 *"Abschrüfft des gelaubens,"* 59v; "Claus Felbinger's Confession," 148.

14 Stuart Murray, "Ecclesiology," in *T&T Clark Handbook of Anabaptism*, ed. Brian C. Brewer (London: Bloomsbury Publishing, 2023), 211.

Mutual admonition is so central to Christian community that the baptismal vows made by every Hutterite include the promise to accept and give admonition. The question posed is: "Do you hereby ask for brotherly discipline and admonition, and promise also to use the same in love where it is needed?" (In German, "*Begehrst du auch, brüderliche Strafe und Anrede anzunehmen und dieselbe auch an andere, wo es Not ist, mit Liebe zu brauchen?*")[15]

Thus, Hutterites are very familiar with the language of "*onredn, wornen und strofn*," which roughly translates to "admonish, warn, and discipline." Note that all these terms suggest that members are called to respond with correction when another member sins. In my experience, many Hutterites, especially our older members, understand this obligation primarily as a responsibility to address wrongdoing whenever it occurs, and commonly experience a sense of guilt when they fail to admonish the offender immediately. This is reinforced by warnings such as this one found in the so-called *Solz-Lehr*[16] based on Matthew 5:13:

> My brother and my sister, what happened to your vow, what happened to your promise, which we publicly pledged in the covenant of baptism, before God and the congregation, that if we do see somebody do something wrong, we will admonish and warn them?[17]

Another *Lehr* that interacts with this phrase is *die Fußwaschung Lehr*, a homily based on the foot-washing scene found in chapter 13 of

---

15 *Im Weinstock treu bleiben: Hilfsquelle für Hutterische Täuflinge / Abiding in the Vine: Resources for Hutterian Baptismal Candidates*, rev. ed. (MacGregor: H.B. Book Centre, 2022), 42–43, Question #8.

16 *Solz-Lehr*, "salt-homily." *Lehr* (literally "teaching") has a dual meaning in the Hutterite tradition. It refers both to an exegetical homily text (*Leadn*, pl.) and to the formal Sunday morning worship service in Hutterite communities, which typically includes communal singing, a thematic and an exegetical homily, and prayer.

17 Traditional Hutterite homily on Mt 5:13b. Hutterite homilies remain primarily preserved within the Hutterite manuscript culture rather than formal published volumes. While the core canon of these homilies has long been established and remains stable, multiple collections copied by different copyists are in common use. This results in slight textual variations and presents challenges for consistent citation. Collections of Hutterite homilies, to varying degrees of completeness, are held across various archival repositories in both Europe and North America.

John's Gospel. The homily addresses listeners in the voice of Jesus, urging them to practise mutual admonition:

> If I, the Master and Son of God, have brought you such a blessing, your salvation, with earnestness and faithfulness, and have desired to remove your misfortune and error in every way, so you should also demonstrate it to one another in every way.

> For this is the highest devotion, blessing, and love, that one seeks the well-being of another. Even if someone does not want to accept it at first, like Peter, he will surely learn to accept it. This should and must be the case with the faithful and the pious: if someone sees his friend and neighbour going astray and falling among murderers, should he not warn him?

> Therefore, the Lord God has given His people every command to keep watch and guard over their neighbours, *with brotherly discipline, warning, and admonition.*[18]

Several other examples could be cited, but this should suffice to establish that this language is common and familiar in Hutterite texts and in Hutterite ways of thinking about mutual admonition and our life together. In short, Hutterites tend to have a narrow understanding of what mutual admonition entails.

I want to be clear that church discipline and mutual admonition do include responding to wrongdoing around us with sensitivity and love, but they are not limited to that. A healthy community has many other habits and practices woven into its fabric to instruct, guide, and direct its members, and to encourage accountability.

I find the phrase "giving and receiving counsel" to be a helpful substitute or supplement to "*onredn, wornen und strofn*" because it refocuses the attention from responding to specific offences toward

---

18 Traditional Hutterite homily on Jn 13:1–38, known colloquially as *die Fußwaschung Lehr*, or the foot-washing homily. Following this passage are references to Mt 18:15 and 7:4 (emphasis mine).

a broader responsibility to engage in the harder work of ongoing discernment, fellowship, and instruction.

So what exactly do I mean by giving and receiving counsel? Giving and receiving counsel can include any means of sharing wisdom in the form of life experiences, questions, insights, guidance, and advice, whether through words or witness, whether privately or publicly, to help each other grow into the full stature of Christ.

Paul on Prophesying

One way to think about this is to consider the word used by the apostle Paul when speaking in chapter 14 of 1 Corinthians about the gifts of the Spirit: prophecy. We are used to thinking of prophecy as primarily about predicting the future, but the term is more accurately understood in the sense of speaking the truth to build up the community. The older German word for prophecy is *weissagen*—literally, "speaking words of wisdom" for the sake of the other. Following his famous chapter devoted to the centrality of love in the life of the congregation, Paul instructs the Corinthians about the priority of spiritual gifts that edify the larger fellowship as opposed to those that promote personal edification:

> Pursue love and strive for the spiritual gifts, and especially that you may prophesy. For those who speak in a tongue do not speak to other people but to God; for nobody understands them, since they are speaking mysteries in the Spirit. On the other hand, *those who prophesy speak to other people for their building up and encouragement and consolation.* Those who speak in a tongue build up themselves, but those who prophesy build up the church. Now I would like all of you to speak in tongues, but even more to prophesy. One who prophesies is greater than one who speaks in tongues, unless someone interprets, so that the church may be built up.[19]

Notice that Paul's language of sharing gifts for the edification of the community is similar to what we heard from Felbinger earlier.

---

19   1 Cor 14:1–5.

It turns out that this was a popular text early Anabaptists looked to for guidance on how to think about how their congregational gatherings should be organized.

An anonymous Swiss Anabaptist publication from the 1530s describes the order of worship in this way:

> That all things may be done in the best, the most seemly and convenient manner when the congregation assembles, which congregation is a temple of the Holy Spirit where the gifts of inner operation of the spirit in *each* one (note, in each one) serve the common good. Note, for the *common* good."[20]

The writer goes on to approvingly quote Paul's teaching on what church gatherings should look like: When they come together, "every one of you (note, every one) has a psalm, has a doctrine, has a revelation, has an interpretation."[21] The expectation is that believers will actively participate in sharing wisdom in a variety of ways.

Finally, the writer asks, rather pointedly: "When someone comes to church and constantly hears only one person speaking, and all the others are silent, neither speaking nor prophesying, who can or will regard or confess the same to be a spiritual congregation, or confess according to 1 Corinthians 14, that God is dwelling and operating in them through his Holy Spirit with his gifts, impelling them one after the other in the above-mentioned order of speaking and prophesying?"[22]

In a similar vein, Hans Umlauft asks: "How can it be a Christian congregation … when no one may openly speak after another and present his gifts and revelations clearly before the people for their improvement?"[23]

---

20 Walter Klaassen, ed., *Anabaptism in Outline: Selected Primary Sources* (Harrisonburg: Herald Press, 1981), 126.

21 1 Cor 14:18–20.

22 Klaassen, *Anabaptism*, 126.

23 Klaassen, *Anabaptism*, 127. Little is known about Hans Umlauft. He was a shoemaker and an effective communicator, baptized by Georg Hueter, a missionary associated with the Hutterite community at Austerlitz in Moravia. See Werner O. Packull, *Hutterite Beginnings: Communitarian Experiments during the Reformation* (Baltimore: Johns Hopkins University Press, 1995), 147.

The active participation of all Anabaptist believers in communal life and worship is based on the conviction that "God is dwelling and operating in [all of] them through his Holy Spirit with his gifts." For Hutterites, this sense of participation is extended to all areas of life, because our whole life together is an expression of our love for God and neighbour.

Prophesying in Acts

In the second chapter of the Acts of the Apostles, Peter explains the miracle of languages to the bewildered crowd by quoting Joel 3. Through the prophet, God had promised to "pour out my Spirit upon all flesh" and that both "your sons and daughters shall prophesy."[24] The description of the new Spirit-generated community that follows is punctuated with references to being together, depicting a community that practises "prophesying" as an act of sharing spiritual wisdom and counsel for the flourishing of the fellowship.[25]

* * 2:42: "They devoted themselves to the apostles' teaching and fellowship (*koinonia*), to the breaking of bread and the prayers."

* * 2:44: "All who believed were together and had all things in common."

* * 2:46: "Day by day, as they spent much time together in the temple, they broke bread at home..."

At the risk of sounding redundant, Luke's account highlights the table fellowship and *koinonia* quality of the first Christians, and suggests that prophesying is one of the marks of the Spirit's presence in the gathered community.

---

24 Acts 2:17.

25 It is worth reflecting on why Luke provides two accounts of the shared life in the new Pentecost community, and how the two accounts differ. Is this an echo of the two creation stories in Gen 1 and 2, intended to highlight the creation of God's new humanity, the church? While the account in Acts 2 emphasizes the whole shared life of the new community (fellowship; Greek: *koinonia*; *Geistes-gemeinschaft*), the account in Acts 4 emphasizes the communal ownership of property (*Güter-gemeinschaft*). Does Luke's placement of these two accounts perhaps underscore the fact that *Geistesgemeinschaft* is foundational and primary and that *Gütergemeinschaft* is derivative and secondary?

The "One Another" Quality of the Gospel

Another way to gauge the importance of mutual edification is to pay attention to how the New Testament speaks about congregational life. The biblical scholar and theologian Gerhard Lohfink has observed that the phrase "one another" (Greek: ἀλλήλων, *allēlōn*) occurs about one hundred times in the New Testament letters, indicating the priority of relationships, community, and mutual edification for the people of God.[26] To be caught up in the spirit of Jesus is to be unavoidably caught up in the life of being with one another in a particular way.

Here are a few examples from five different New Testament letters. Note the different ways God's people are called to serve one another.[27]

* Galatians 6:2: "Bear one another's burdens, and in this way you will fulfil the law of Christ."

* 1 Thessalonians 5:11: "Encourage one another and build up each other."

* James 5:16: "Confess your sins to one another, and pray for one another, so that you may be healed."

* Hebrews 10:24–25: "And let us consider how to provoke one another to love and good deeds, not neglecting to meet together, as is the habit of some, but encouraging one another, and all the more as you see the Day approaching."

* Romans 15:5: "May the God of steadfastness and encouragement grant you to live in harmony with one another, in accordance with Christ Jesus."

* And an example from John 13:34–35: "A new command I give you: Love one another. As I have loved you, so you must love one another. By this everyone will know that you are my disciples, if you love one another."

Lohfink writes: "Proper admonition requires much of the one who admonishes, for instance, the courage to allow oneself to be cor-

---

26 Gerhard Lohfink, *Jesus and Community* (Philadelphia: Fortress Press, 1982), 99–106.

27 See also Rom 14:19; Heb 3:13; 1 Pet 4:8.

rected on another occasion, and the knowledge that in a truly fraternal community conflicts absolutely must be resolved, not suppressed or artificially concealed. The courage to admonish others fraternally and the humility to let oneself be corrected are among the most certain signs of the presence of authentic community."[28]

The Church's Mission

Felbinger's description of the church community would have been incomplete if he had not mentioned, albeit briefly, the church's overall purpose or reason for existing. Ultimately, the reason believers are called to give and receive counsel is to show the world how God wants all people to live; that is, to call all people to repentance and new life:

> For God still has an obedient people on earth, whom he has startled from sin through his living Word, called by his holy name, separated from the world, and gathered through his Holy Spirit. He desired this people as his own, to the praise of his glory, that they may live according to his nature, proclaim his power and virtue, adorn their faith with godly works, put on the cloak of justice and innocence, and always wear the breastplate of right action, *so that the world can see what is pleasing to God, consider and abandon its ungodly life, and to turn from sin to God.*"[29]

In other words, giving and receiving counsel also has important implications for the church's mission of sharing the Gospel, and for how we relate to our friends and neighbours beyond our local community.

Conclusion

I hope a few things have become clear. Early Anabaptists and Hutterites like Claus Felbinger understood that at the heart of the

28 Lohfink, *Jesus and Community*, 106.
29 "*Abschrüfft des gelaubens*," 74v; "Claus Felbinger's Confession," 155. Emphasis mine. Compare Peter Riedemann, *Peter Riedemann's Hutterite Confession of Faith*, trans. and ed. John J. Friesen (Waterloo: Herald Press, 1999; Walden: Plough Publishing, 2019), 77–78.

Christian faith is a new way of relating and communing, a new way of being together where love and mutuality is the operative principle.

This new way of relating goes far beyond the common understanding of church discipline as being primarily about addressing wrongdoing, and includes the more comprehensive practice of giving and receiving counsel, of encouraging and building up one another through the sharing of gifts.

Giving and receiving counsel is essential for instructing members in the way of Jesus, and for the church to be a witness to God's new humanity.[30]

Hutterite life, then, is best understood as an attempt to live out the Gospel by radical sharing, not just of our possessions, but of our whole lives.

In the next lecture, we will take a closer look at the different forms of giving and receiving counsel that are important to lived Hutterite experience, and consider areas where our life together may be enriched by leaning more courageously into the biblical and theological insights we have been exploring.

Questions for Discussion & Reflection

* What impressions do you have about early Anabaptists' convictions and practices around the sharing of gifts within the church community?

* How does your experience of and thinking about life together compare with what Felbinger is describing?

* How do you understand the vow or expectation to "admonish, warn, and discipline?" How have you experienced it?

---

30   Eph 2.

If, then, there is any comfort in Christ, any consolation from love, any partnership in the Spirit, any tender affection and sympathy, make my joy complete: be of the same mind, having the same love, being in full accord and of one mind. Do nothing from selfish ambition or empty conceit, but in humility regard others as better than yourselves. Let each of you look not to your own interests but to the interests of others. Let the same mind be in you that was in Christ Jesus,

> who, though he existed in the form of God,
>> did not regard equality with God
>> as something to be grasped,
> but emptied himself,
>> taking the form of a slave,
>> assuming human likeness.
> And being found in appearance as a human,
>> he humbled himself
>> and became obedient to the point of
>> death—even death on a cross.

PHILIPPIANS 2:1–8

LECTURE TWO
Building the Body with
Mutual Admonition Today

"How have you come to faith? We want to hear your story." This was a question one of my Sunday-school students asked me this past year. We were reading Zacchaeus's conversion story as part of a study of salvation and the new birth; I had explained how, like Zacchaeus, Jesus is calling each of us down out of our lofty position in the tree, looking us in the eye, joining us at home for coffee, and inviting us to change our lives.

"What is your story?" the student wanted to know. "How does your experience map onto the story of Zacchaeus?" For a moment, I was not sure how to respond. My initial instinct was that sharing my faith journey would be somewhat presumptuous, perhaps even arrogant. How could I honestly tell this winding, complicated story from where I stood? Wasn't it more appropriate that other people interpret my story, and tell me how I had changed? How would I avoid falling prey to self-delusion?

Yet the more I thought about it, the more I realized I owed my students an account—however imperfect—of how I have come to faith and the ways in which I have grown so far. Besides the biblical and historical witnesses, they needed to see and hear stories of the living God at work transforming the lives of the people around them, including—and perhaps especially—the adults entrusted to nurturing them in the faith. I share this anecdote as an example of how I have received counsel from one of my students, and how it has helped me think about our responsibility as parents and teachers, as brothers and sisters, to speak into the lives of our young people with care and intention in order to support their spiritual formation.

In this lecture I want to probe how and where we are giving and receiving counsel in our communities today and how we might enrich and extend this practice. I will draw on my experiences as a Sunday-school teacher and brother (i.e., someone who has taken on the responsibilities of full membership) in my local community, simply because it is what I know best. I do this with some reservations, because it's personal and unique to my context in many ways. Every community is different. What I will share is intended to provoke reflection and conversation about what might be appropriate for your context and for your community.

To begin with, I'd like to take an inventory of sorts about where Hutterites traditionally are expected or encouraged to share their wisdom with each other. Where do we already do a decent job of this? First, it must be acknowledged that a lot of giving and receiving counsel goes unnoticed, under the radar, in the privacy of personal conversation; perhaps most importantly, it happens in the quiet walks or hidden lives of brothers and sisters who don't say much, but live out their faith in compellingly consistent, beautiful lives.

It also happens in other more public and structured ways:

* It happens at the daily meeting of *Rot*, the place where we come to seek and share counsel about travel plans, special requests, or concerns, and to discuss business decisions. The word *Rot*, after all, means "counsel." It makes a world of a difference whether we understand *Rot* as a space for asking permission from superiors or as a forum for giving and receiving counsel among brothers and sisters.

* It happens when we meet in our homes following *Lehr und Gebet*[1] to discuss the themes that were raised, or when we visit with our extended family or with guests to talk about things that matter to all of us.

---

1   *Gebet* ("prayer") denotes the shorter, more frequent evening services held during the week, which emphasize prayer, singing, and a continuation of the Sunday homilies.

* It happens at an *Aufred Hulba*, the engagement celebration a week before a wedding, where brothers—and increasingly sisters—are expected to share wisdom with the couple based on their life experience about how to tend to and nurture a marriage so it can flourish to benefit the larger church community. This exchange of insights not only benefits the young couple; it provides us an opportunity to reflect on the state of our own marriage covenants. I understand the practice we are familiar with today is fairly new, perhaps thirty or forty years old, and that the way it is experienced varies considerably, but is a practice that we have come to cherish.

* It happens at *Erkleadn*[2] when we express gratitude or remorse to the congregation, and it happens during the two weeks of preparation, throughout which we are encouraged to reconcile with our brothers and sisters so we can participate in the meal of remembrance with a glad heart and good conscience. It happens, too, when members meet to discuss how to respond to and hold accountable a member who has confessed a serious sin.

* It happens when our baptismal candidates meet with community elders during the seven Sundays prior to baptism; in recent years, our conference leadership has encouraged more members to get involved in this process.[3]

* It happens when a brother or sister is appointed to a new position in the community. Usually, the leaders—and increasingly other members—are invited to share some words of counsel, an *Aufmunterung* that will help the brother or sister do well in his or her job.

---

2   *Erkleadn*, German, *Erklären* ("to declare"), is a Hutterite practice occurring two weeks before Easter, in which baptized brothers—and in some communities, also the sisters—publicly declare their intention to participate in good conscience in the annual observance of the Lord's Supper.

3   Arnold Hofer, Samuel Waldner, and Josh Hofer, "Conference Report" (ecclesial encyclical, March 11, 2022), 6, pt. 5, "On Leading Well."

* It happens at the annual or quarterly financial meetings (*Virlesn*), or at budgeting meetings, where we wrestle with how to best steward the community's resources.

* It happens when we encourage or comfort one another through singing, whether it be around a campfire or via HBNi livestreams.

* These days, it also happens through WhatsApp statuses and various online support groups.

There are other examples that could be mentioned, but this will suffice to make the point that the giving and receiving of counsel is already happening in many ways, and I think we would all agree that our communities would be impoverished indeed if this was not the case. However, my sense is that we are not realizing the full potential for giving and receiving counsel or spiritual mentorship in our communities, especially in the form of intentional, structured spaces that support the spiritual formation of our youth, mutual admonition and instruction among adult members, and the strengthening of intergenerational bonds through community-wide exchanges. I say "spiritual" with some hesitation, because I don't want to suggest that this happens only when we discuss the bible, or that it doesn't happen when we wrestle with more mundane things like how to organize our work schedules or how to make good financial decisions. As a people who believe that our whole life is infused with the yeast of faith, we want to remember that the spiritual is woven into every aspect of our life together under the Word.

In this lecture, I want to explore how we might enrich and extend our practice of giving and receiving counsel in two areas: the spiritual formation and discipling of our youth, and wrestling together with scripture and our faith experiences.

Spiritual Formation and Discipling of Our Youth

Let's return to my Sunday-school class for a minute to consider what giving and receiving counsel might look like in that context. One of my students recently reminded me that discipleship isn't just about wise, mature adult believers faithfully following the way of Jesus. It is also about older members intentionally mentoring, guiding, and discipling younger members in the Jesus way, through word and deed, through giving and receiving counsel. How do we do that? Again, I want to emphasize that the most important way this happens is when there is a compelling witness or experience of a living faith in a loving congregation. Without that, no teaching can be convincing or winsome: "By this everyone will know that you are my disciples, if you love one another."[4] Having said that, part of being a living body is giving thought and intention to how we guide, direct, and nurture our young people into the faith.

The goal of Sunday school is, of course, to nurture and cultivate the faith of our youth. I have been teaching students aged fifteen and up for about ten years, and one of the things I have learned over this time is the need to balance explicit teaching (about scripture, prayer, the Apostles' Creed, the catechism, etc.) with attentiveness to the questions and struggles my students bring to class.

Our youth are facing a number of significant challenges that have consequences for faith formation: Many of them are immersed in a digital culture that is distracting, highly addictive, and anxiety inducing. In general, they are better educated than the previous generation, which means they have more questions and higher expectations for the spiritual and intellectual quality of communal life. They are encountering ideas, including forms of faith and lifestyle options, at an unprecedented rate, and they are affected by the larger ethos of fragmentation and loss of hope in the West.

In short: The waves of modernity, with its celebration of individual autonomy and freedom from traditional constraints, are washing onto the Hutterite shores, and the walls of separation we used to rely on for protection are no longer adequate. Our youth will need a strong adult presence and guidance to navigate and survive these waters.

In a survey I conducted recently, one of my students expressed her desire for a more intentional form of discipleship:

> I feel deeply that there is a lack of intentional discipleship targeted at young and older believers.

---

4   Jn 13:35.

Having mature Christians ask us meaningful and thought-provoking questions, and being there to guide us if answers fail us, is something I generally feel is lacking. On top of this, teaching us how to read the bible in a productive and fruitful way is almost non-existent. Too often, I feel that I have to reach to YouTube sermons, books, and podcasts to answer these questions.[5]

How can we respond to this hunger, to this need? How can we provide more guidance to our youth, given the challenges they face?

Demonstration #1: Student Conferences

I'd like to share an example of how I have tried to be more intentional with how I mentor our youth. About three years ago, I began meeting individually with each of our *Buem und Diene*,[6] face to face, usually following Sunday school. My motivation was very simple: How could I minister and speak into the lives of my students if I did not know their struggles, their questions, their joys, and their sorrows—if I didn't attend more closely to their experiences? How could I be a sensitive *Seelsorger* (spiritual caregiver) if I didn't have a sense of the state of their souls? I have a class of about thirty, so my goal is to meet with each student at least once a year, and as many as three times each year.

I make a point of telling them that we are not meeting because they are in trouble, or because I want to punish them, but simply so I can check in on how they are doing and ensure they are learning what they need from me. I call these meetings "check-ins."

What do I ask them about? Again, this is something that continues to evolve, and I am still learning a lot, but here are some of the things we usually talk about:

* I ask them about their spiritual nourishment habits, including their prayer life, scripture reading, and conversa-

---

5   Author's survey conducted in May 2025, in author's collection.
6   *Buem und Diene* is a common Hutterite term referring to young people in the community—*Buem* (boys) and *Diene* (girls)—typically unmarried young adults fifteen and older.

tions about faith. I offer advice about how to better structure that part of their life so they can build healthier habits.

* I ask them whether *Lehr, Gebet,* and Sunday school is serving them well and if they have any adjustments or topics to suggest.

* I ask them about their friendships, their social life. If I know there is a significant other, I'll ask about how they are navigating that. I share advice from my experience, affirm the gift of sexual desire, but also draw attention to how it needs to be disciplined and directed.

* I ask them about their habits concerning technology, screen time, alcohol, consuming music, lust and pornography, and the like. I assure them that no matter what their addiction, speaking about it and bringing it to light breaks its power—especially if someone they trust can assure them of Christ's forgiveness and help keep them accountable.

* I ask them about how they understand faith, whether they have felt the call of Christ on their lives, whether they find their life in Christian community compelling or attractive, and if they understand how they can grow in faith. Recently, I had a conversation with a student who had returned after leaving the community and was trying to understand the process of reacceptance.

* I ask them about their goals, short-term and long-term, including their goals for baptism.

* I don't ask every student the same questions. I make some mental notes about things I want to talk about, but leave room for flexibility, depending on how the conversation goes.

* If required, I loop in parents, and on some occasions I try to facilitate further professional support.

I have been pleasantly surprised at how meeting with students has allowed me to speak into their lives as an older adult, to learn from them about what they need from me as their teacher and about how they understand faith and the world (It's been a while since

I was fifteen or twenty!). This routine has helped me to pay more attention to what is happening in their lives, so I can speak into their world more effectively and sensitively. I consider transitions and rites of passage like turning fifteen and graduation from high school. I make note of recent trips, challenges and successes, new jobs, and changing family or community dynamics. I also give students a year-end survey to see what they are finding helpful and where they need more support.

I offer this description to draw attention to the fact that as a community of counsel and care, we need to be intentional about how we are forming and discipling our youth, and we need to be there for them in very concrete, personal ways. The form this will take will depend to some extent on your context, but the need for counsel is very real for all of our youth. I also assume and recognize that I am one of many people in my community, including parents, who are doing this work in a variety of ways. This is not work a Sunday-school teacher can do on his own.

It's also important to teach students to give and receive counsel among themselves.[7] One way I teach them about this is to have classes about once a month that are organized as a "sharing circle," in which each student gets the opportunity to say something in response to a prompt. For example, on Good Friday this year, we read John's account of the crucifixion with several pauses where students could record something they heard in the story about who God is and who humans are, or anything else that was new and interesting to them. Following the reading, each student was invited to share an insight or question as we passed the talking stick around the circle. Not only is this a way to get almost 100 percent participation, and thus a form of accountability (no one is off the hook, although they can pass if they have nothing to say), it is also a way for students to grow in their ability to have something significant to contribute to the learning community and to express it with confidence and thoughtfulness. They learn to hear and receive counsel from a variety of perspectives and experiences, and not just from the teacher.

---

7   I don't mean to suggest, however, that young people should turn to each other for advice when dealing with adult-sized problems.

We also have a regular prayer practice (about once every six weeks) where students write down two things that happened in the last week or two on an index card: First, they name an experience in which they felt the grace or goodness of God at work in their life (gratitude), and second, they name a misstep—a time when they missed the mark or experienced their own brokenness, a moment when they felt pain or sadness (confession). Then, I invite them to share one or both of these experiences with a partner; sometimes, I'll expand it to a small group of three to five, and sometimes we will gather in a sharing circle so we can hear some of their glad and sad moments as a large group.

A warning: If you are just starting out with this practice, be patient and recognize that it will take time to develop trust. In fact, as the teacher, you will need to model openness and vulnerability by sharing personal experiences many times before students will venture forth. You will also need to create a safe, open space so students feel comfortable taking risks and sharing about their personal lives.

In addition to my student-life antenna that pays attention to what is going on in students' own lives, these two practices (the sharing circle and the prayer practice) help to inform who I meet with for a one-on-one conference after any given class. I collect and read students' prayer cards (with permission), and this, too, helps me to know what they are celebrating and struggling with.

Here is what some of my students shared about their experience in one-on-one conferences: "As someone who puts her walls up when someone forces guidance and unwanted life advice on me, I truly treasure the times people take to be real and present with me." Another student described how being seen and heard through these conversations opened up a deeper spiritual path: "I appreciate how you ask questions nobody else does. It makes me feel seen and heard, which is something I struggle a lot with from many other people in my life. When I was in the worst spot ever, those talks made me go do something about it. I turned to prayer as my biggest tool, and saw the results of giving things to God and asking for his strength almost immediately. And that made me want more and more of the same feeling of being happy every day and able to enjoy everything I had to do, instead of just focusing on the negatives every day." Another recalled a shift over time, from resistance to trust: "When I was younger, I used to find the one-on-ones like an interrogation. I thought the questions were too personal. But recently I was struggling with something and I came to you because I knew you would listen (which is already a lot) and give me the tools to power through, and with the help of God and friends, my problem could be fixed." And one student reflected on the power of presence itself: "The example you set by investing your time for us goes far beyond anything that any person could ever tell or attempt to teach us."[8]

Wrestling Together with Scripture and Our Faith Experiences

The next arena for giving and receiving counsel I want to consider is regarding how we wrestle with scripture and how we talk about our faith experiences and questions with one another.

There has been a fair bit of discussion in recent years about the place of our traditional *Leadn* in the life of the community.[9] This is a complex issue that I can't delve into very deeply here, but I do want to consider one common concern around this topic. There is a growing sense that, whether or not our traditional teachings are communicating clearly to our people, there is a need for a public space to discuss not only the Sunday sermons, but questions and insights around faith and scripture in general. Where do we have a structured public space to give and receive counsel around issues of faith? We do have German school and Sunday school where youth can interact with an adult about spiritual concerns (usually the same person), but there is a definite gap for baptized and older members, and very few structured opportunities for intergenerational exchanges. While there is a lot of religious instruction in our

---

8   Author's survey conducted in May 2025, in author's collection.
9   Kenny Wollmann, "Creed and Confession," unpublished presentation notes, February 2025, in author's collection. See also Arnold Hofer, Josh Hofer, and Jonathan Wollmann, "Conference Report," (ecclesial encyclical, March 4, 2025), 6-7, pt. 5.f., "Hutterite History: Apostles' Creed and Homilies." This is also a recurring topic in adult education sessions I've led, conversations with students and community members, and other similar forums.

society, there appears to be a lack of intentional spiritual mentorship for youth, especially once they turn fifteen.

Early Gatherings

This hunger for a deeper engagement with scripture has parallels in early Anabaptist history. As discussed earlier, a core commitment of many Anabaptist congregations was the active participation of all members in worship and bible reading.

When we think about the early Reformation period, we sometimes imagine that the invention of the printing press suddenly made it possible for everyone to read the bible for themselves. The reality is that most people could not read and did not have access to a copy of the bible. Typically, it was literate craftsmen or clergy who read out loud to a gathered assembly. In many ways, this is how believers have encountered scripture since the days of the early church. The big difference was that now the reading was in a language the common people understood! We can safely assume that these gatherings would have included many questions and vigorous discussion about the meaning and application of the text, especially in light of the expectations for the order of worship among Swiss Anabaptists described earlier.

The earliest communal order of 1529 found in the Hutterite *Chronicle* gives us some clues about what community gatherings were like in the early years. You may recall that the first community was established at Austerlitz in Moravia in 1528, when the *Stäbler* were expelled from nearby Nicolsburg. Some scholars date this *Ordnung* to 1527, but the first Hutterite chronicler, Kaspar Braitmichel, inserts it at the beginning of our movement, suggesting it was a foundational document for the early Hutterites. Remarkably, five of the twelve points in this document (almost half!) focus on issues related to gathering as a community. Let's look at a few of them:

Point #1 emphasizes the importance of the community gathering to pray for each other and to discern God's will for their life together: "When the community gathers, we should wholeheartedly pray to God for grace so that he reveals to us and makes known his divine will. When parting ways, we should thank God and pray for all the brothers and sisters in the entire Christian community."[10]

Point #2 suggests that frequently gathering as a community is seen as a way to "encourage one another," indicating a form of worship that was more participatory: "We should encourage one another in a heartfelt and Christian way to remain steadfast in the Lord, gathering often—at least four or five times during the week, if possible, whether with half or the entire congregation."[11]

Finally, Point #7 emphasizes that the speaking and sharing at the gatherings must be done in an orderly manner and must be disciplined and edifying: "At community gatherings only one should speak and the rest listen and judge what is spoken, and not two or three standing at once. No one should curse or swear and pursue idle chatter so that the weak are spared."[12]

Two other points in the *Ordnung* deal with topics we've already touched on. Point #3 outlines the "rule of Christ" for disciplining members in the church community: "If a brother or sister lives outside the order, this should be addressed publicly before the community with gentle admonition. If it is a private [offence], it should be disciplined in private, but according to the command of God."[13]

Point #4 reinforces the idea that life in Christian community involves the whole person and is not simply about relinquishing control of one's money and possessions: "Let every brother and sister commit themselves fully and wholly to the community, *yielded to God with body and their whole life*. All gifts received from God should be held in common according to the practices of the first apostolic church and community of Christ so that the needy in the community are supported like the Christians in the time of the apostles."[14]

---

10   Jesse Hofer and Kenny Wollmann, eds., *For God's Truth: A Hutterite History Reader* (MacGregor: Hutterian Brethren Book Centre, 2024), 112.

11   Hofer and Wollmann, *For God's Truth*, 112.

12   Hofer and Wollmann, *For God's Truth*, 113.

13   Hofer and Wollmann, *For God's Truth*, 112–113.

14   Hofer and Wollmann, *For God's Truth*, 113 (emphasis mine).

Together, these points tell us a few things about the early Hutterites:

1. Gathering as a community, which likely looked very different than what we would call *Lehr und Gebet* today, was central to their common life;

2. All members were invited to share their wisdom in an orderly manner; and

3. There were challenges with gathering that needed to be addressed so things would run smoothly.

Bible Reading in Hutterite History

According to scholar Martin Rothkegel, the Hutterites were the only sixteenth-century group that was able to realize the widely shared Reformation goal of universal lay reading of the bible. They supplied a New Testament to every baptized member, and a complete bible was made available in workshops and other public buildings.[15] Although we have little evidence of what bible reading and discussion looked like in daily life, the evidence we do have suggests a lively conversation between members around faith and the application of scripture.

Through the process of institutionalization in the latter half of the sixteenth century, the early model of reading and wrestling with the bible as a community developed into a more or less "closed canon" of *Leadn* or homilies. At least some of our *Leadn* began as bible commentaries, likely intended as a resource to be used by ministers for sermon preparation.[16] By the early seventeenth century, in the context of declining discipline and education, excerpts from these commentaries were read verbatim, as they are to this day.

Several hundred years later, in the early nineteenth century, elder and chronicler Johannes Waldner lamented changes to public reading and discussion of the bible at the community at Radicheva in

---

15 See Martin Rothkegel, "The Living Word: Uses of the Holy Scriptures among Sixteenth-Century Anabaptists in Moravia," *Mennonite Quarterly Review* 89 (April 2015).

16 See Hauprecht Zapff, *Johannes der Evangelist über alle Kapitel erklärt: Ein Bibelkommentar von 1597*, ed. Martin Rothkegel (MacGregor: H.B. Book Centre, 2017).

Russia. This practice had apparently been introduced by Mathies Hofer, one of the Carinthian crypto-Protestants who were incorporated among the old Hutterites in Transylvania in the 1750s. Their piety was more emotional and expressive, and they brought with them the memory of having to secretly read and discuss the bible in the privacy of their homes back in the Klagenfurt region of Catholic Carinthia. Mathies was responsible for introducing other divisive practices, and one can hear a certain ambivalence in Waldner's report—but also a clear sense that a valuable practice had been lost:

> After brother Hans Kleinsasser passed away and Mathies Hofer left the community, the practices introduced by him also gradually began to fade and disappear, which I don't want to altogether commend or celebrate. For the practice of praying together and especially reading [the bible] together after lunch, where everyone took a turn, was edifying and useful for the youth. Often, a discussion ensued about the meaning and application of a passage of the Holy Scriptures. Each person developed the ability to fluently read the Holy Scriptures, and this practice could still be practiced today with a good conscience. Now, every young brother wants a well-bound Bible with large print, and many (the diligent exempted) know little about its contents. Paul teaches us in 1 Thessalonians 5: "Test everything and keep what is good." Thus, one could have omitted what was unnecessary and excessive, but kept what was good. Each can judge this matter for himself.[17]

One of the challenges that persist today is to find a way to organize structured public encounters with the bible that yoke the wisdom and maturity of older members with the burning questions and ex-

---

17   A.J.F. Zieglschmid. *Das Klein Geschichtsbuch der Hutterischen Brueder* (Philadelphia: Carl Schurz Memorial Foundation, 1947), 354; translated by the author. Cf. also *The Chronicle of the Hutterian Brethren*, vol 2. (Ste. Agathe: Crystal Spring Colony, 1998), 504–505.

uberance of the youth, and to do so in a way that allows the Gospel to challenge the status quo while avoiding chaos and disorder.

Demonstration #2: Open-Mic Community Sharing

Next, I want to share a bit about our community's experience with publicly discussing issues related to faith and scripture. About two years ago, we began experimenting with having an open microphone following the Sunday lunch meal. This grew out of a growing recognition among our leaders and the community as a whole that we lacked a space to talk together about our experiences of faith and our encounters with scripture. At that point, we had a fair bit of experience with talking together in various forms, including a weekly Saturday meeting in the shop involving all the men involved in the workforce, structured discussions around technology use involving men and women aged fifteen years and up, and various other meetings. I've described this in more detail elsewhere if you are interested.[18] Please keep in mind that we have been practising having structured conversations as a community in various forms for over twenty years.

So what does this look like, and what have we learned from this open-mic practice? Following the noon meal and the singing of the youth choir or the whole congregation, our leaders open the floor for comments or questions. Our ministers take turns moderating the discussion, which usually involves giving brief remarks or posing a question based on the *Lehr* or the singing. Then, people have the opportunity to share an insight, a question, an experience, a word of encouragement, or a challenge. On a typical Sunday, three to eight people will share an insight for between five and twenty minutes. Often, people comment on the *Lehr* message, both affirming and extending it, or raising questions about it. Sometimes, people report on a trip or a significant experience; other times we discuss a concern such as breakfast attendance, dress code, or seating order.

---

18   Jesse D. Hofer, "Building Capacity for Communal Conversation: Gemeindeordnungen and Discernment in the Hutterite World," in *Navigating Tradition and Innovation: Essays Commemorating the Permanent Settlement of Hutterites in Manitoba*, ed. Kenny Wollmann (MacGregor, MB: Hutterian Brethren Book Centre, 2024), 321–45. This essay is also included in this publication as an appendix.

Some people speak regularly, some people never speak, and once in a while a new voice has the courage to enter the conversation. Those who always have lots to say learn to moderate their voice, and those who are reluctant learn to step out in faith to share their gifts with the community. We are still learning and growing into this. A young person recently posed a question following the *Lehr* message on preparedness for baptism: "What evidence are you looking for when you consider whether a young person is ready for baptism?" This prompted several older members to respond.

Not every Sunday is the same. Sometimes, the mood is flat and not much is said, especially when we have consecutive holidays. It is important to acknowledge that not all days are the same, and not to be discouraged by this. This practice requires effective moderation and vulnerable leadership. Leaders don't have to have the last word or the only word, and they do need to lead by giving people space to express their voices in a way that builds the community. Effective moderation means briefly setting the stage by posing an appropriate question or giving a short summary of the topic, then standing back and giving space for other voices to enter the conversation.

Personally, this practice has made me more aware of my responsibility to at least occasionally have something to share, and has made me listen more attentively at *Lehr und Gebet*. It has made me more conscious and attentive to what our community is going through and how I might respond to these challenges. Above all, we have experienced this weekly sharing of insights, questions, and interpretations of the scriptures from men and women as life-giving and healthy. Often, the experience is so rich that I postpone Sunday school to Monday evening, because I feel like we have just had an intergenerational exchange that I can't match in Sunday school! Where else do we have a space to do this?

Again, I share these details not because I expect you to do exactly what we are doing, but to encourage reflection about how your communities share wisdom across the generations, and how this might be extended and enriched. This can take many different forms. For example, I am aware of a community that hosts regular book-club meetings where they read and discuss a variety of texts dealing with the joys and challenges of community life, and another community that organizes regular, voluntary meetings to discuss issues of common concern, like how to have a good discussion or how to cultivate gratitude. Yet another community has regular, structured bible studies where older and younger members gather to read and discuss scripture. In one community, baptismal candidates have not only recited the traditional *Taufspruch*[19] prior to baptism, but have shared a personal story about how they came to faith.

Here are a few responses from my students about how they have experienced the open-mic sharing in our community: "I love the open-mic as it gives everyone in our community a voice. It has helped me see and feel how the body of Christ should function, and I've begun to see it as a form of worship."

"The sharing as a community has helped me glimpse what it looks and feels like to be a part of the kingdom of God. People listening to each other, weighing each other's opinions, and sharing personal insights about God is just beautiful. It has set a higher standard for what community means and is. It affirms our need to live out our faith together. It showed me that I cannot be a Christian alone. It has helped me see the responsibility of living in a Christian community called to live in right relationship."

"It encourages me to think about my own faith journey, and also to talk about my faith, not just keep it to myself. It is meant to be shared. [This sharing] has also made me see some of the members in my community differently. They are on the same road I am, and have so much wisdom to share!"

"It has taught me that a community can live in peace and unity within diversity. It is beautiful to be open and honest with each other, to be able to connect with each other, but still, in the end, have a common goal and continue to live in peace."[20]

---

19 Each baptismal candidate recites a 190-line poem titled "*Ein schöner Spruch für die Täuflinge zu lernen* [A poem for the baptismal candidates to learn]." See *Im Weinstock treu bleiben: Hilfsquelle für Hutterische Täuflinge / Abiding in the Vine: Resources for Hutterian Baptismal Candidates*, rev. ed. (MacGregor: H.B. Book Centre, 2022), 20–33.

20 These responses come from a survey of Sunday-school students conducted by the author in May 2025, in author's collection.

As these comments make clear, this exchange of wisdom between young and old is teaching our youth significant lessons about the rewards and responsibilities of being part of the body of Christ.

Conclusion

I want to briefly highlight some principles that can guide our giving and receiving counsel:

* **Servant leadership is essential.** Effective leadership is not about having all the answers or making all the tough decisions, but about leading a team of diverse people gifted by the Spirit of God who can share the load that the body is meant to bear together. The main task of leadership is to provide the community with a clear vision, rooted in the way of Jesus, and to create ways and means to pursue this vision together. Do our leaders create sufficient space for all members' voices to be heard and respected, to cultivate a climate where challenging conversations can take place? Are our members willing to accept the responsibility that goes along with this?

* **Learning to converse respectfully as a community takes time, patience, and practice.** Active listening, effective moderation, discerning when to share, organizing one's thoughts, building on what others have said, and clearly expressing one's thoughts are skills that need to be patiently nurtured.

* **The best learning and teaching take place in the context of connection and healthy relationships.** Do we take the time and care to nurture deep, meaningful relationships, to build the necessary trust and space—what I like to call the relational capital—to make our words carry weight? Trust is absolutely essential for open and honest communication, and open and honest communication builds trust and encourages vulnerability. Trust, of course, has to be built over time and grows wherever tenderness and truthfulness are consistently practised.

* **Remember the source.** Life in Christian community is nourished and made possible by the grace and power of God, particularly what God shares with us in the life and spirit of Jesus. When we lose sight of this basic fact, we often resort to rigid rule following, bullying, and manipulation to enforce our vision of community, and our giving and receiving counsel is done, if at all, in a spirit of fear and compulsion.[21] Can we remember that our life together is rooted in the gospel of grace offered through the person of Jesus Christ,[22] so we can be freed to give and receive counsel in a spirit of vulnerability and mutual trust instead of rigidity and hostility?

In their discussions of life together in Christian community, both Claus Felbinger and Hans Schmied allude to Proverbs 25:11–12 to describe the treasure of a fitting word of wisdom shared among the faithful:

> A word fitly spoken
> is like apples of gold in a setting of silver.
>
> Like a gold ring or an ornament of gold
> is a wise rebuke to a listening ear.[23]

This image is a reminder that wise counsel is fitting and beautiful, and when it is humbly accepted, a wise rebuke is a precious gift.

The traditional Hutterite *Lehr* on Philippians 2 presents a fitting illustration of mutual support in Christian community: When a herd of caribou cross a river, the strongest takes the lead in fighting against the current, and each animal in turn places its head on the back of the caribou in front, to benefit from the strength of the herd as a whole. Nobody is left behind. When he is tired, the leading caribou goes to the rear and lets others lead the way. This

---

21 Cf. Dietrich Bonhoeffer, *Life Together* (Minneapolis: Fortress Press, 2015), 9–10: "Those who love their dream of a Christian community more than the Christian community itself become destroyers of that Christian community even though their personal intentions may be ever so honest, earnest, and sacrificial."

22 Phil 2:5–11.

23 Cf. *Güldene Aepffel in Silbern Schalen, oder schöne und nützliche Worte und Wahrheiten zur Gottseligkeit* (1702), a popular devotional book of the Swiss-Mennonite Brethren.

illustration underscores the fact that we need each other to survive the perilous pilgrimage of discipleship and that the responsibility of care is shared by all. It reinforces the commitment made in the waters of baptism, where—taking our lead from Jesus Christ—we vow to serve each other through word and deed.

Discussion Questions

* How does your community intentionally mentor or disciple its youth? How does your community wrestle together with the interpretation of scripture?

* What other practices has your community adopted that have enriched the giving and receiving of counsel?

* What obstacles and opportunities for giving and receiving counsel do you see in your community?

APPENDIX
Building Capacity for Communal Conversation: *Gemeindeordnungen*[1] and Discernment in the Hutterite World

On January 30, 2018, Schmiedeleut Group I pastors and stewards met at Acadia Community for the first conference since Arnold Hofer was elected *Ältester* (elder) on August 30, 2017.[2] The principal issue on the agenda was how to proceed with the conference's broken relationship with Schmiedeleut Group II.[3] In 1992, the Schmiedeleut Conference of the Hutterian Brethren suffered a painful schism that led to the creation of separate constitutions and church conferences.[4] In the years since 1992, much of Group I's ecclesial energies had been devoted to navigating the aftermath of the division. Of particular concern were the policies surrounding intermarriage and interaction between the two groups.

At the inaugural January conference, participants had the opportunity to speak about the issue for several hours in an open micro-

---

1   *Gemeindeordnungen* are communal orders or regulations designed to guide or instruct members of the church community. Synonyms include: orders, regulations, ordinances. In some ways, *Gemeindeordnungen* are similar to monastic orders, such as the Order of St. Benedict. Traditionally, *Gemeindeordnungen* are made and revised at an annual conference of ministers. In this essay, I will use *Ordnungen* as a shorthand for *Gemeindeordnungen*.

2   All male Schmiedeleut members vote to elect an elder. The ordained minister with the most votes becomes the new elder. A meeting is held, usually at the predecessor's community, to announce the new elder.

3   Arnold Hofer and Samuel Waldner to "*alle Gruppe 1-Schmiedenleut Hutterer-Gemeinden in Manitoba, Kanada; Minnesota, Nord und Süd Dakota, USA* [all Group I Schmiedeleut Hutterite Communities in Manitoba, Canada; Minnesota, North and South Dakota, USA]," January 15, 2018.

4   See Ian Kleinsasser, "Voices of Conflict: A Perspective of the 1992 Schmiedeleut Church Schism" in this publication for a more detailed account of the church division.

phone format. Following the sharing of personal reflections and the exchange of diverse viewpoints on how best to proceed on this issue, it was decided that the church[5] would initiate a policy of "cautious openness" toward Group II communities in an attempt to cultivate a healthier relationship between the two groups. In addition to opening the floor for participants to express their concerns, questions, and longings, *Ältester* Arnold Hofer emphasized the need for leaders to initiate and lead conversations with their respective congregations about this issue.

A Call for Communal Discernment

Several days after the conference, Arnold Hofer reminded ministers about their responsibility to initiate discussions in their local communities about how the church division had been handled in their respective case:

> This brief letter is a reminder that I have requested that all ministers should address their communities in a spirit of openness about how our group has dealt with the division in the past twenty years. I want to encourage you and all our brothers and sisters to share what is on their hearts without fear of repercussion. Particularly I am concerned with how we as *Prediger* have had to draw hard lines; where this was done with unkind words toward our brothers and sisters—the sheep we are tending— let us lead the way and say, "*Es tut mir Leid.* [I am sorry.]"[6]

The fact that this reminder was sent out so soon after the conference highlights the significance of this point for the church's leaders.

The instruction that leaders communicate with their congregations about issues addressed at a church conference is not new. Elder Arnold Hofer's predecessor, Jacob Kleinsasser, who served as elder from 1978–2017, frequently urged his fellow "servants of the Word" to communicate church policies and decisions to their com-

---

5   "Church" is used here for simplicity's sake to denote the Schmiedeleut Group I Conference of the Hutterian Brethren.

6   Arnold Hofer to [Schmiedeleut I] ministers, February 3, 2018.

munity members, although in many cases, his exhortations seem to have fallen on deaf ears. What is new in this church memorandum is that it makes it incumbent upon ministers to lead discussions in their respective communities about how they have dealt with the issue of the church division in general, and in particular, how they have treated members with respect to visiting rights for Group II relatives. The assumption is that some leaders have not dealt wisely or sensitively with this matter and they are expected to acknowledge this and change their ways. It is also noteworthy that actions which may have been seen as a sign of faithfulness earlier, namely taking a stand for the church, are now being called out as a problematic abuse of power. For close to twenty-five years, many ministers had acted as gatekeepers who enforced church policies around shunning in their respective communities, often without much community-level dialogue; now, their actions were being called into question by new church leadership. Clearly, these developments reflect an important shift in Schmiedeleut I church polity and deserve careful attention and reflection.

The February communication was followed about a month later by the official conference report, which reiterated the need for congregational-level dialogue and discernment with respect to the church division:

> Ministers are reminded of their important assignment clearly outlined in the letter dated the third of February 2018. It stated that each community must have its own discussion on how members stand in regard to the state of affairs with our church division and, where needed, repent for slander, lovelessness, and injustice. Ministers, in particular, have the task to listen with open hearts and gentleness because they have an important responsibility toward those who experienced pain and trauma due to the division. This openness will make the way to reconciliation and healing possible in cases where power and authority were unwisely wielded and abused.[7]

---

7   Arnold Hofer and Samuel Waldner to "all Hutterite communities of Schmiedeleut

Building on the February document, the official report goes further by highlighting the need for renewal through effective leadership, communal dialogue, self-examination, confession, and repentance. Ministers are reminded that they have a special responsibility to listen to their members and acknowledge hurts and injustices, especially with respect to the handling of the policy of *Meidung* in connection with the church division. The emphasis on grassroots discussion is seen as fundamental for paving the way for reconciliation at the church level.

There is much to celebrate and affirm about these developments at the Group I Conference level. First, it is encouraging to see the tradition of *Gemeindeordnungen* in the form of a conference letter addressing the broader Hutterite church being revived, albeit in a modified form and tone. There is a noticeable shift away from specific rules governing behaviours to general exhortation and instruction that invites further reflection and discussion. While the church's tradition of guiding its members through annual *Gemeindeordnungen* at the conference level is not without its problems, the absence of *Gemeindeordnungen* is arguably even more problematic. Second, the official conference report draws attention to the significant issue of how Hutterite *Prediger* understand and exercise leadership, an issue that has been plaguing the church for some time.[8] Leaders bear a special responsibility to regularly communicate church issues and policies to their congregations, as well as to initiate and facilitate discussion about issues of common concern. Unfortunately, some leaders used the period of uncertainty and instability following the 1992 schism to shore up their power, leaving many members indifferent and deeply disillusioned with their leaders and communal life. Finally, the emphasis on involving the wider church membership—the brothers and sisters who comprise the church, the body of Christ—in meaningful congregational-level discernment and conversation is an encouraging development.

Group I…," Schmiedeleut Group I Conference Report, March 8, 2018.

8   Leonard Gross to "the Dariusleut, Lehrerleut and Schmiedeleut," May 19, 1993. See also Peter Riedemann's letter addressing the issue of "double honour" in early Hutterite congregations in *The Chronicle of the Hutterian Brethren*, 200–209.

Despite the hopeful tone and message of the 2018 conference report, some significant obstacles stand in the way of its implementation to any meaningful extent. It is difficult to imagine how the church's recent shift in policy can have the intended effect when many of its leaders lack the necessary skills or inclination to invite open conversation and wider participation within their congregations. In the rest of this essay, I will explore how an unhealthy or deficient culture of discussion and discernment within many communities will likely conflict with the recent policy of "cautious openness" in the Schmiedeleut Group I Conference with respect to how their communities wrestle with the church division. Part of the challenge confronting the church is a recent shift in the form and function of the *Ordnungen*, which have provided moral guidance since the beginning of the Hutterite movement; navigating this transition well is of utmost importance. Several biblical and theological reasons why conversation is vital for the life and witness of the church will be examined. Finally, a number of examples and practical suggestions for developing a stronger, healthier culture of discernment will be considered. It is my hope that this can become a starting point for rich discussions around these vital questions as we seek to be more faithful witnesses to the *Gemeinschaftsleben* (communal life) that God is calling us to.

Evolution of *Gemeindeordnungen* among Hutterites

In 1527, Swiss Anabaptists met at the border town of Schleitheim to debate and discuss the common convictions they shared in the dynamic early years of the Anabaptist movement. The outcome of the conference was a document known as "Brotherly Union," or the "Schleitheim Confession," one of the earliest Anabaptist orders. Its purpose was to seek unity among a minority movement in danger of fragmentation and to provide practical guidance on how Anabaptist believers and communities ought to order or conduct themselves.

Early Hutterites followed this example of writing church ordinances to establish an orderly community life. One example is the Community Order of 1529, which outlines, among other things, how leaders should serve the needs of the people, how members should be disciplined, and how *Gütergemeinschaft* (community-of-goods) should be practiced.[9] Significantly, the seventh point in the Order deals with how to conduct healthy conversations as a community: "At community gatherings only one should speak and the rest listen and judge what is spoken, and not two or three standing at once. No one should curse or swear and pursue idle chatter so that the weak are spared."[10] From the beginning, Hutterites recognized the importance of effective communal conversation.

As the charismatic leadership of the Jakob Hutter era (1533–35) was gradually formalized and institutionalized, *Gemeindeordnungen* became more prominent. The earliest *Schulordnung* was produced in 1558 under Leonard Lanzenstiel and updated numerous times by Peter Walpot (1565–78) in 1568 and Hans Kräl (1578–83) in 1578.[11] Its purpose was to instruct schoolmasters and schoolmothers on how to properly care for the children in a boarding school context. The *Kuchlordnung* regulated the roles in the communal kitchen and gave dietary guidelines for different groups of people. Kräl described the late-sixteenth-century Hutterite mindset with respect to *Ordnungen* in this way: "There has to be order in all areas for the matters of life can be properly maintained and furthered only where order reigns—even more so in the house of God whose master builder is the Lord himself. Where there is no order there is disorder. There God does not dwell, and the house soon collapses."[12]

---

9   See Werner Packull, *Hutterite Beginnings*, 33–37. Although the Hutterite *Chronicle* dates it to 1529, Friedmann argues for an earlier date. In any case, it is significant that this Order (also known as the Church Discipline) and not the Schleitheim Confession was included in what eventually became *Das Große Geschichtsbuch*, the first volume of *The Chronicle of the Hutterian Brethren*. However, the Schleitheim Confession was included in at least one Hutterite codex. See Josef von Beck, *Die Geschichts-Bücher der Wiedertäufer in Oesterreich-Ungarn [Schriften der Wiener Akademie der Wissenschaften]*, F.R.A. 2, 43 (Vienna, 1883), 41–44.

10 *The Chronicle of the Hutterian Brethren*, vol. 1 (Rifton: Plough Publishing House, 1987), 78. The original found in *Das Große Geschichtsbuch* reads: "*Zum siebenten: In der Gemein Versammlung soll Einer reden, die andern zuhören und richten, was geredt wird, und nicht zwei oder drei zusammen stehn. Keiner soll fluchen oder schwören und daß kein unnütz Geschwätz getrieben werden, auf daß der Schwachen verschont werde*," 61.

11 The earliest *Schulordnung* was produced in 1558 under Leonard Lanzenstiel (1542–65). See Martin Rothkegel, "*Die älteste Schulordnung: Ein Ordnungszettel von 1558*," *Mennonitische Geschichtsblätter* 55 (1998), 85–105.

12 *The Chronicle of the Hutterian Brethren*, vol. 2 (Ste. Agathe: Crystal Spring Colony, 1998), 761.

Throughout the sixteenth and seventeenth centuries a number of new *Gemeindeordnungen* were produced. Some regulated the work departments, acting as a form of quality control, while others addressed spiritual concerns such as commitment to *Gütergemeinschaft* and non-violence. During his eldership when communities were ravaged by the Thirty Years War, Andreas Ehrenpreis (1639–1662) attempted to reverse the community's decline by writing, collecting, and enforcing a number of these orders.[13] Later Hutterites relied on these church orders to organize their communities and inform their decision-making process. For example, when communalism was revived in Transylvania in the early 1760s, the brothers and sisters "were led to establish and maintain true Christian order for their practical and spiritual life."[14] Among other documents, they looked to the old School Order for direction. Later, when the community in Russia was embroiled in a bitter dispute about the proper mode of prayer, they "searched carefully through our forefathers' writings" for guidance.[15] According to chronicler and elder Johannes Waldner, the purpose of recording the community's conflicts was "to warn against any of us presuming to introduce a new practice he has invented himself and thereby alter, disturb, and displace the old, well-proved order of the church."[16]

As elder, Johannes Waldner showed remarkable openness to other groups, especially the Moravian Brethren. He corresponded regularly with Johann Wiegand, the Moravian minister at Sarepta, and he clearly admired their devotion and piety.[17] Writing as the official Hutterite chronicler in about 1781, Waldner lamented the breakdown of the order of worship introduced by *Ältester* Hans Kleinsasser and the departure of Mathies Hofer:

> I do not mean to commend this neglect, nor am I glad for it. The gatherings for prayer and especially the reading at midday helped build up the young

---

13   Wes Harrison, *Andreas Ehrenpreis and Hutterite Faith and Practice* (Kitchener: Pandora Press, 1997). See especially Chapters 3 and 4.

14   *The Chronicle of the Hutterian Brethren*, vol. 2, 393.

15   Ibid., 493.

16   Ibid., 495.

17   Astrid von Schlachta, *"Holding Fast to What is Good? Tradition and Renewal in Hutterite History,"* trans. Jesse Hofer (MacGregor: Hutterian Brethren Book Centre, 2020), 41–42.

people's faith. As previously described, each read in turn and so each was involved, and it often led to a talk about the meaning of a passage of Holy Scripture. At that time each one took pains to be able to read out the Scriptures fluently, and such a practice could still be used with a good conscience today. Now each young brother wants to have a good, well-bound Bible with big print, but many of them (always excepting the zealous) know little of what is inside. Paul taught in 1 Thessalonians 5:2, "Prove all things hold fast to what is good." It would have been possible to drop what was unnecessary and exaggerated and to keep what was good. But each can judge the matter as he sees fit.[18]

This passage clearly shows that Waldner was able to critically evaluate how the church's orders impacted the spiritual life of the church community, and he was confident that the community could have discerned a prudent way forward.

In the twentieth century, Hutterite church orders increasingly focused on the minutiae of dress code, home furnishing, and technology; overall, they sought to limit contact with the non-Hutterite world and cultivate an ascetic piety. In the second half of the twentieth century, both *Ältester* Joseph Kleinsasser (served 1967–1978) and *Ältester* Jacob Kleinsasser (served 1978–2017) resisted creating new *Gemeindeordnungen*. Instead, they favoured a policy of moral instruction and intrinsic motivation or conversion that is closer to the philosophy of chronicler Johannes Waldner (served 1794–1824), who observed, perhaps somewhat nostalgically, "Regulations for daily work were not present in the beginning nor were they necessary since each member in a right, simple, and child-like spirit, served God and the devout with all faithfulness and each gave freely of his entire ability."[19] A well-known proverb

---

18 *The Chronicle of the Hutterian Brethren*, vol. 2, 504–505. The first three sentences of this passage appear in all caps, suggesting an emphasis by the author.

19 *The Chronicle of the Hutterian Brethren*, vol. 2, 761. This quotation contrasts with the one cited in footnote 16. Perhaps one reflects the outlook of a younger, more idealistic leader and the latter, the thought of a leader who has experienced considerable upheaval in his community. In this essay, I use Hans Kräl and Johannes

among Hutterites is that it takes more wisdom to write a new *Ordnung* than to observe it: "*Es get herter eh gueta Ordnung mochn, as wie ahna holtn* [It is more difficult to make a good ordinance than to maintain one]."

It could be said that the tension between Kräl's emphasis on external order via communal ordinances and Waldner's emphasis on the spiritual basis for an orderly communal life was one of the factors that contributed to the 1992 Schmiedeleut church schism. In general, Schmiedeleut Group II has emphasized the use of ordinances to regulate dress, technology, and home furnishings, while Group I has been more drawn to education and missions as the means of moral formation. For Group I, the upheaval and destabilization caused by the schism and a different understanding of the purpose and utility of *Gemeindeordnungen* resulted in less energy devoted to organizing annual conferences and drafting new *Ordnungen* and increasing attention to managing the boundaries between the two groups through policies surrounding intermarriage and boundary maintenance.[20] Since 1992, with the exception of policies dealing with interaction with Group II, Group I has produced virtually no ordinances that provide guidance in other important areas of church life such as leadership, material wealth, sexual ethics, education, and issues related to technology. This shift was widely welcomed by Group I members, many of whom were unhappy with what they perceived as legalism and over-regulation through top-down church legislation.

A lack of formal discussion and guidance on these pressing moral issues is not a development that ought to be welcomed by a Christian people. The new reality without regular church ordinances made room for individual congregations to make more decisions locally, which might have presented an opportunity to develop lo-

---

Waldner as representatives of two ways of thinking about *Ordnungen* and as two possible ways forward for Hutterites today. The historical characters very likely would not correspond neatly to this dichotomy, since the historical reality is always much more complex than such a sharp dualism would allow. Indeed, one can see how in some ways, Waldner was very cautious and conservative, while in other respects he was open to new ideas and willing to try new things to inspire the community he led.

20 For example, Jacob Kleinsasser, "*Bericht von der Konferenz* [Conference Report]," July 30, 1997, in author's collection.

cal discernment skills.[21] In reality, however, the change meant that each community was left to grapple with these challenges more or less on its own, which resulted in a growing level of disconnection or disunity between many communities.[22] The election of a new elder and the drafting of new conference letters under his leadership represents an opportunity to recognize the deficiency of an order-less church on one hand, while acknowledging the unhealthy, legalistic over-regulation which ruled in the church for much of the twentieth century on the other. This is the time to give congregations more room for local discernment and to equip and form leaders who are courageous and vulnerable enough to be servants of the Word, who facilitate congregational conversations while fostering unity within the broader church.[23]

However, it is one thing to revive the tradition of writing church orders to assist local congregations in their discipleship and faith formation, and quite another challenge to cultivate the conditions for holding healthy discussions in local congregations. Grassroots[24] participation in creating church and perhaps congregational orders is another approach worth exploring. This would require discussion

---

21 Unfortunately, in most communities this did not happen, which is not surprising, because in many communities both community leaders and brothers and sisters have been socialized to obediently follow their leaders without asking questions and without the benefit of open dialogue. As such, members are not schooled in the discipline of participating in essential communal conversations. Often, this is justified by references to the baptismal vow of obedience and the related posture of *Gelassenheit*. Instead, in many cases, leaders took the opportunity to become the main agent of decision-making, which helps to explain our leadership problem today.

22 Some communities formed informal alliances where leaders did things in similar ways; others were left alone until problems erupted. There are some benefits to this lack of conference pressure; local autonomy limits the coercive nature of broad church policies that may be the work of a vocal minority.

23 Brené Brown, *Dare to Lead: Brave Work. Tough Conversations. Whole Hearts.* (New York: Random House, 2018). See especially Part I, "Rumbling with Vulnerability," which addresses a number of common myths associated with vulnerability, contrasts daring and armoured leadership, and explores the relevance of shame and empathy for leadership.

24 The fact that I'm distinguishing between "grassroots" and "leadership" levels in our communities suggests an existing, problematic divide or distance between many of our leaders and the people they are charged to lead. We would do well to recover our confidence in Jesus' promise that all believers are empowered to participate in discernment: "Where two or three are gathered in my name, I am there among them" (Matthew 18:20).

within each congregation about its vision and priorities and would invite greater participation in the life of the church. When drafting new *Ordnungen* of a more general, hortatory nature, the conference might find a way to hear from a representative cross-section of members on a given policy using surveys and other tools. Addressing the culture of communal conversation will be crucial to the effectiveness of any new *Ordnungen* that are produced, especially if the content of the orders requires communal dialogue in the first place, as the January 2018 conference document does.

Diagnosing the Issue

What are the signs that Hutterite communities are suffering from a culture deficient in dialogue as a means of discernment and decision-making at the congregational level? To my knowledge, no formal studies of this question have been made. There are, however, numerous relevant clues, one of which is the financial struggles experienced by many communities. A recent document outlining the implementation of an Economic Stewardship Council among Schmiedeleut Group I reports that as many as twenty-five communities (close to 50%!) are dealing with significant financial challenges.[25] To take an extreme example, in one newly founded community, members were unaware that the community had accumulated $8 million of debt over five years![26] The authors of the economic stewardship document recognize that one of the ways to address growing financial troubles in our communities is to facilitate closer communication, not only about the financial status of the community, but also about sustainable living standards.[27] In his report at the 2019 conference, council liaison Jack Waldner cites "on-going concerns such as a lack of accountability and transparency" as one of the main factors contributing to financial mismanagement. "Leaders need to encourage the thorough discussion of issues, plans, and ideas with members before making decisions.

---

25 Hutterite Brethren Stewardship Council Mission Statement, August 2018, in author's collection. Schmiedeleut Group II has organized a similar advisory committee.

26 Arnold Hofer and Samuel Waldner to "Brothers and Sisters in Jesus Christ [Schmiedeleut I membership]," June 18, 2018, in author's collection.

27 Hutterite Economic Stewardship Council Mission Statement, August 2018, in author's collection.

There must always be fair and due process which prevents nepotism."[28]

Furthermore, strong anecdotal evidence suggests that many leaders communicate very little of what gets discussed at conference-level meetings to their congregations, and that they are making more decisions about large purchases without consulting the brotherhood than was traditionally the case. At a meeting of Group I leaders in March of 2019, Elder Arnold Hofer told ministers, "In my analysis of the challenges our church is facing today, I have come to believe that a lack of good communication, disrespect, and the disunity that comes from this, is increasingly separating us."[29] If that is true, it is difficult to imagine the same leaders initiating discussions over complex and controversial issues.

There is another important reason why it is imperative that Hutterite communities develop a healthy culture of conversation. As we react to the rapidly changing economic and technological landscape, we find ourselves navigating another shift of seismic proportions in our communities—the changing face of education. Since the late 1990s and the advent of the Brandon University Hutterian Education Program (BUHEP), close to 100 teachers have graduated from universities in Brandon and Winnipeg and are teaching in their local communities. As a result, we have produced a generation of high school graduates who have been taught to think, question, and discuss issues at a level that is foreign and even intimidating to the older generations. The significance of this development for the culture and internal dynamics of Schmiedeleut Group I communities cannot be overstated. For the first time in their history, a significant number of individuals were sent to university in the hopes of taking back the responsibility of educating their own children.[30]

---

28 Arnold Hofer and Samuel Waldner to "all Hutterite communities of Schmiedeleut Group I in Manitoba, Canada; Minnesota, North and South Dakota, USA," "Schmiedeleut Group I Conference Report 2019," 5.

29 Arnold Hofer, "Concerning Leadership in our Communities." Speech notes for H.B. Mutual Shareholders' meeting, March 28, 2019, in author's collection.

30 Shortly after emigrating to the United States of America, about a dozen Hutterites took a year of education in neighbouring colleges and taught in their respective colony schools. About half a dozen Hutterites received their teachers' training between 1970–1990. The numbers that graduated from 1999–2015 is simply unprecedented in Hutterite history.

What many community leaders did not anticipate, however, were the unavoidable tensions and growing pains that would result from new ideas and ways of thinking chafing against traditional beliefs and cultural norms, especially in a context where the necessary conditions for conversations were not adequately cultivated.[31]

Without a robust culture of conversation, these developments in the Hutterite education system hold great potential for misunderstanding, alienation, and disunity. Many older members do not consider that encountering new ideas at university for five years will (and should!) inevitably change anybody. What else is the point of attending an institution of higher learning? To learn is to be changed. The challenge for each community is to bring the wisdom of the community's tradition into dialogue with the best ideas learned by its members at university through ongoing, honest conversations. Clearly not everything learned at university will be beneficial to the community; members who attend university need help digesting, filtering, and metabolizing what they learn so they can help build up the community. Members who have had the luxury of studying history, literature, psychology, sociology, philosophy, theology, and other subjects, may have some helpful, albeit painful, critiques for their community and the wider church. As I have already noted, teachers or other members gifted in facilitating conversations can also play a role in leading communal discussions that will support this process.

At the same time, university-trained members will need to be sensitive to the fact that they have had the benefit of reading, learning, and interacting with diverse conversation partners over several years and have been changed in significant ways as a result. Other community members have not had the same experience and will naturally be at a very different place in their thinking. Regularly reflecting on one's intellectual development is one way to cultivate awareness and humility in this regard, because it is a reminder that

---

31   Two unpublished papers that show some awareness of these challenges are Raymond Kleinsasser, "Hutterite Education: Growing Pains" (MA thesis, University of Manitoba, 2007) and Tim Waldner, "Hutterites and High School: Do they Match?" (2000). While the people who were pushing for higher education were willing to challenge the status quo and welcomed the changes it would bring, many others were less prepared for the adjustments.

absent the reading and learning we have been privileged to experience—to say nothing of the patience and generosity shown to us by our teachers and conversation partners—we would think and talk in ways similar to the people whose logic we may reject.[32]

These brief forays into the economic and educational realities Hutterites are navigating show why they would benefit from developing practices and cultures that encourage community-level conversations that promote transparency and help to bridge differences. Next, we turn to consider why conversation should matter to people of faith.

Conversation in the Body of Christ

The words community and communication share the Latin root *communis*, which means "shared by all" or "to have in common." A healthy community exists when members have a shared sense of why they are living together. What purpose does our life together serve? What is the church's vocation, and how does it relate to our congregation's priorities? Is it primarily an economic purpose, or is there a larger spiritual vision of achieving wholeness through living out the gospel together and sharing that witness with the world? Conversation can help a community reflect on its vision and assess whether its current practices and priorities are congruent with its stated goals.

One of the most consistent metaphors for the gathered people of God in the New Testament is the human body.[33] This assembly of believers (Greek *ekklesia*) or "called out ones" is also referred to as the body of Christ.[34] Through the church, Christ is bodily present with the world (Matthew 25). In other words, the church is called to embody the ministry of Jesus, to be the healing presence of its Master through the power of the Spirit. As such, the heart of the church's mission is to be salt and light to the world. What does conversation have to do with the church's mission? Conversation

---

32 A useful discussion of this is found in Alan Jacobs, *How to Think: A Survival Guide for a World at Odds* (New York: Penguin Random House, 2014), 123, 144–146.

33 See Eph 2:16 and 4:1–16; Col 3:15; 1 Cor 12:12–31; the famous meditation on love found in 1 Cor 13 appears within a discussion of the spiritual gifts of believers, "so that the church may be built up" (14:5).

34 Rom 12:5; 1 Cor 12:27; Eph 5:23; Col 1:18 and 1:24.

has many practical benefits in the workplace, in family life, and in other social contexts. Its usefulness, however, may have been obscured to many Hutterites by ingrained attitudes and beliefs about leadership, conflict, and the Christian life in general. For example, if we have been taught that conflict should be avoided we will not value the kind of communication skills that are necessary to deal well with conflict. If we have been socialized to believe that our leaders bear the full burden of decision-making, we will be less likely to expect to be consulted about decisions. If we think that Christian discipleship is primarily about following the community's or the church's rules, we will not see the importance of ongoing and active reflection and participation in discernment in order to build up the community. To that end, I want to suggest three biblical and theological reasons why engaging in healthy communal conversation should be taken seriously. All three are deeply rooted in the church's vocation to be a witness and faithful presence to the world. The three features are not meant to be exhaustive. Rather, they are representative of the kind of witness the church should be as it lives out its vocation as the body of Christ.

1. Conversation is Essential for Church Unity

The body of Christ is called to pursue unity. In the Gospel of John, Jesus prayed that his disciples "may all be one," as Jesus and the Father are one "so that the world may believe that you have sent me."[35] The church's unity is both a reflection of the intimate relationship between Father and Son and the Trinity as a whole; and it is an argument for the incarnation, making it possible for people to believe what might otherwise be inconceivable or fanciful. The church's unity is essential because when the church is united, it is more effective in being the hands and feet of Jesus, ministering to a hurting world and pointing people to the good news of his lordship.

There are various examples in church history of leaders and members meeting to talk through difficult issues. One of the earliest examples is described in Acts 15. A controversial issue that divided the early church was how to treat Gentile converts: should they be

---

35　Jn 17:21.

required to practice Jewish law, including circumcision and dietary customs, or should they be accepted simply on the basis of their faith in and allegiance to Jesus? The leaders resolved this thorny question by calling the first church council: they met at Jerusalem to debate the matter and eventually reached a decision that would pave the way for the expansion and flowering of the Christian faith.

As mentioned earlier, the early Anabaptists also convened a conference to work towards unity during the Reformation period. The Swiss and South German Anabaptists met at the Swiss border town of Schleitheim to discuss and work out seven articles that they agreed on. It is worth noting that the document they produced was entitled "Brotherly Union"—an attempt to work for unity in an age of chaos and fragmentation. In the introduction to "Brotherly Union," the author (probably Michael Sattler) declared,

> Joy, peace, and mercy from our Father, *through the reconciling* [vereinigung] *blood of Christ Jesus*, along with the gifts of the Spirit [...] be with all who love God and the children of the light who are scattered about wherever God has deigned to place them and wherever they are gathered in unity in the one God and Father of us all. Grace and peace of heart be with you all.[36]

Unity is not the same as uniformity or conformity; it does not mean that everybody is the same or that everyone agrees about everything. Rather, unity is about being united by the same Spirit to serve the same Lord through the rich and diverse collection of individual members that make up the body of Christ, otherwise known as the church. We can strive for unity by talking about our differences and by discussing our hopes and dreams for our community, instead of secretly gossiping about how we have been mistreated or how somebody made the wrong decision. In this way, we can contribute to the community's welfare and be appropriately disciplined and corrected by our fellow brothers and sisters.

---

36   Jesse Hofer and Kenny Wollmann, editors. *For God's Truth: A Hutterite History Reader* (MacGregor: Hutterian Brethren Book Centre, 2024), 90. Emphasis added. John Howard Yoder notes that "A most significant concept in the thought of Michael Sattler is that of *Vereinigung*."

There is a common misconception that all conflict is unhealthy, or even un-Christian. In fact, conflicts and disagreements are a natural part of human experience. A conflict is an opportunity to deal with an existing problem in an honest, healthy way. What matters is how the conflict is processed or dealt with. A conflict can be avoided, manipulated, angrily confronted, or talked about respectfully, in a spirit of generosity, patience, and forbearance, with the goal of getting to the bottom of the issue at hand. If the church's unity is to help the world believe that God has sent Jesus to save us (John 17), it will need to be motivated by the Spirit of unity expressed in the letter to the Ephesians:

> I therefore, the prisoner in the Lord, beg you to lead a life worthy of the calling to which you have been called, with all humility and gentleness, with patience, bearing with one another in love, making every effort to maintain the unity of the Spirit in the bond of peace. There is one body and one Spirit, just as you were called to one hope of your calling, one Lord, one faith, one baptism, one God and Father of all, who is above all and through all and in all (4:1–5).

Working for unity in the church has always been challenging. Today, unity is threatened by a polarized political climate and by individualism in the West. Now more than ever the world needs the witness of Christ's body gathering in humility to seek unity through gracious conversation.

2. Conversation is Essential for Reconciliation in the Church

Reconciliation is at the heart of the gospel and the church's vocation (Matthew 5:9; 2 Corinthians 5:16–21; Romans 5:1–11). "In Christ," Paul writes to the Corinthians, "God was reconciling the world to himself" (19). Those who are "in Christ" are a "new creation" called to serve in the ministry of reconciliation as "ambassadors for Christ." They share and embody the message that through Christ, God is reconciling the world to himself.

Problems with communication are a major contributing factor in most conflicts. Often, conflicts and misunderstandings erupt as a result of a failure to communicate honestly, clearly, and charitably. Sometimes conflicts happen when people do not listen patiently enough or do not watch their words carefully enough. When we learn to communicate in a timely and open manner, and when we learn the necessary skills to dialogue well, we become better equipped to prevent conflicts and better able to resolve them once they happen. This is especially important for Hutterites, who live in close proximity to their brothers and sisters and because of their commitment to Christian community.

The rule of Christ found in Matthew 18:15–20 recommends a redemptive process for resolving conflicts and is premised on the ability of brothers and sisters to talk frankly about difficult matters. This was a favourite text for early Anabaptists and remains foundational for how the church understands conflict resolution. The familiar promise of God's presence "where two or three are gathered in my name" assumes that believers will be people who meet in a variety of ways to address broken relationships and to discern what is essential for ongoing faithfulness. "Truly I tell you, whatever you bind on earth will be bound in heaven, and whatever you loose on earth will be loosed in heaven. Again truly I tell you, if two of you agree on earth about anything you ask, it will be done for you by my Father in heaven. For where two or three are gathered in my name, I am there among them."[37] This passage appears in a chapter devoted to teachings and parables about forgiveness and reconciliation, suggesting that God is present in a special way to those who meet to talk about issues that divide them.

3. Conversation is Essential for Discernment and Moral Formation in the Church and is Consistent with the Theology of Believer's Baptism

The early church theologian Tertullian once observed, "Christians are made, not born." Often we assume that most of the formation into the Christian life happens prior to baptism. In reality, disciple-

---

37   Mt 118:18–20.

ship is a life-long process of growing into the fullness of Christ in the context of the believing community.

Believer's baptism assumes that when regenerated, believing men and women are incorporated into the body of Christ through baptism, and are therefore responsible for contributing to the body's welfare and wellbeing. Hutterite baptismal vows include a promise to give and receive admonition to keep the body honest, to help it grow in a healthy manner, and to ensure that its witness is effective. At the same time, young disciples need ongoing guidance and nourishment to grow into their faith and mature in their discipleship. Giving and receiving admonition is not simply an obligatory, spur-of-the-moment response to a misstep or sin, but an invitation to conversation in order to encourage or counsel a brother or sister in need of direction, ideally in the context of a cultivated relationship.

Baptism is also a commitment to share the struggles and glories of the body of Christ, particularly those of one's local congregation. Paul writes to the believers at Rome that God's Spirit reminds them of the glorious fact that they are children of God and joint heirs with Christ, "if in fact, we suffer with him so that we may also be glorified with him" (Romans 8:14–17). This pattern of cross and resurrection is, of course, patterned after the life of Jesus and is basic to Paul's understanding of the Christian life. Involving members in sharing the burden of making difficult decisions so they can take responsibility for the community's future is a way to help them mature as believers and participate in the work God is doing through the local congregation.

Hutterites are very familiar with the descriptions of the life of the early believers in Jerusalem found in the Acts of the Apostles. Acts 2:44–45 and 4:32–35 in particular are pivotal texts, because they describe how the early believers practiced community-of-goods in response to the outpouring of the Spirit of God. Another striking feature of the early Christian communities described in Acts is their commitment to be together in fellowship (German *Gemeinschaft*; Greek *koinonia*). This section in Acts begins with the description "When the day of Pentecost had come, they were all together in one place." Once the Spirit pulsed through the gathered believers, they were moved to change their lives in a radical way. Besides economic sharing, "they devoted themselves to the apostles' teaching and fellowship, to the breaking of bread and prayers" (2:42). "Day by day, as they spent much time together in the temple, they broke bread at home and ate their food with glad and generous hearts" (2:46). While *Gemeinschaft* is often associated primarily with economic sharing (*Güter-gemeinschaft*), its meaning refers to the dynamic togetherness and mutual support experienced by believers who share the same Spirit and worship the same Lord. The purpose of the fellowship among believers is no doubt multi-faceted, but surely one reason for it is to encourage growth and understanding among believers through edifying conversation.

To reiterate, learning to talk within the body of Christ is essential for the growth and maturity of its members, who are thereby knit together in love and equipped to better serve each other and the world through mission.

> But speaking the truth in love, we must grow up in every way into him who is the head, into Christ, from whom the whole body, joined and knit together by every ligament with which it is equipped, as each part is working properly, promotes the body's growth in building itself up in love (Ephesians 4: 15–16).

In the final section we will consider examples of several practices that hold potential for developing greater capacity for robust conversations in our communities.

Practices for Nurturing Dialogue Skills and Encouraging Participation

One of the issues confronting Hutterite communities in recent years is how to develop guidelines around the wise use of technology, particularly smartphones and the internet. While some *Leut* groups have responded to this challenge through legislation (i.e., creating new *Ordnungen*), the Schmiedeleut Group I's approach has—intentionally or otherwise—left each community to develop its own policy.[38] In this section I will describe the process of discernment my home community of Silverwinds, Manitoba, went through as we wrestled with the challenges surrounding technology. Along the way I will reflect on what lessons this experience might offer for recovering a stronger culture of dialogue and discernment, both at the congregational and conference levels.

The internet, computers, and cellphones made their appearance in Silverwinds gradually and innocently enough. Their first sanctioned use was as business tools whose utility was difficult to argue against, since they were an economic benefit to the community—the traditional, though by no means foolproof, Hutterite litmus test for adopting new technologies. In the early 2000s, when flip phones were used primarily as communication devices for travellers, our community shared five cellphones. Around 2008, all baptized brothers received a personal cellphone, but only brothers in leadership positions in the various work departments subscribed to a data plan. Internet access was available to adults mostly through desktop computers at the school computer lab, which was designed with transparency and mutual accountability in mind. Content was filtered and access shut off at 9:00 p.m. Youth received an internet account once they graduated and had demonstrated a certain level of maturity; students who wished to use the internet had to be signed in and monitored by teachers. There were some discussions among the teachers and parents in those early days about how best to manage the evolving ecosystem of online access, but very little dialogue was happening formally at the community level.

With the advent of the smartphone and Wi-Fi, the urgency for a wider communal conversation and clearer policies increased. Now, anybody with a digital device and a password could access the internet. Several other potential changes appeared on the horizon around 2016: smartphones for female members and blanket Wi-Fi across the community.[39] To help us wrestle with the bundle of

---

38 One exception is the establishment of Hutterian Broadband Network Inc. (HBNi) initiative, a church organization that provides filtered internet to many Hutterite communities.

39 In general, gender roles in Hutterite culture are traditional and patriarchal: the men are active in managerial and bread-winning roles in the community's barns,

difficult questions surrounding our use of technology, our *Rot*, or community council, appointed a committee to organize a series of meetings.[40] As older leaders, they recognized that they were not in the best position to lead a conversation around technology use, so they delegated the responsibility to younger members who were more familiar with the technical details and who were more capable of facilitating the discussion. This delegation of responsibility was crucial to the success of the process and required courage and vulnerability from our leaders. The process was built on a relationship of mutual trust and goodwill, which has to be cultivated on an ongoing basis. Of special note is that several members of the planning committee were teachers.

With respect to issues in the wider church, how can the church delegate responsibility to members who have the necessary gifts, so that they can deal with complex questions and issues more effectively, instead of assigning somebody a task because he is already in a leadership position?[41] How can trust and goodwill be effectively nurtured and nourished among our leaders and between leaders and the people they lead?

At our first community meeting we did two things: we reviewed the current situation and policies with respect to digital access in our community and gave participants (anybody fifteen years or older) a chance to raise questions and concerns around the use of technology. The committee planned several opportunities over the course of the meeting for participants to talk with each other in small groups in order to build trust in the process and in each other, to

---

shops, and fields, while the women assume responsibility in the domestic sphere. The earliest justification for personal cellphones as a business tool meant that access for women came about a decade later, when it was taken for granted that cellphones were also vital for communication purposes.

40   Our community used a similar approach when dealing with the challenges surrounding COVID-19 beginning in the spring of 2020. A committee was appointed to review provincial regulations and safety recommendations from the Hutterite Safety Council's COVID-19 Task Force, discuss and implement a plan for ensuring the community's compliance with these regulations, and to regularly communicate changes to our members.

41   Three examples where this is already happening are the Hutterian Broadband Network Inc. initiative, the H.B. Stewardship Council mentioned above, and the Hutterian Safety Council, an inter-*Leut* committee tasked with spearheading safety policy and programming.

develop discussion skills, and to give everybody a chance to hear from their group members and voice their own thinking. This process was important, because people are not born with the ability to participate well in discussions or to exercise discernment. Communication skills are learned, and we learn best through guided practice. Too often we take for granted that people should be able to have quality discussions without ample time and opportunity to exercise or practice the necessary skills. How can we create time and space for discussions—both at the congregational and conference levels—in order to involve more people in decision-making and discernment around crucial issues so that the community can benefit from the diverse gifts among us and to wrestle together with how to be faithful Christians today? This challenge takes on a new urgency at a time when conversations are especially threatened by the highly attractive and addictive, but socially non-demanding, low-investment culture of digital communication.[42]

After having several opportunities to talk, small groups sorted their technology questions and concerns into categories such as "Effects of Technology on Child Development" and "Technology and Conscience Formation" and "Social Media Concerns." As a large group we brainstormed categories and narrowed them down to a manageable number. Questions of a technical nature were addressed first because they were the easiest to answer. Further research and investigation were needed to answer many of the questions, and participants were invited to volunteer to prepare presentations to help the community learn about the different aspects of technology use.

In a series of four follow-up meetings the presentations were shared, often by a team of two or more presenters, in an attempt to deepen the learning and potential discernment regarding technology.

---

42 For a sustained and insightful treatment of this topic, see Sherry Turkle, *Reclaiming Conversation: The Power of Talk in a Digital Age* (New York: Penguin Press, 2015). I think here of WhatsApp groups, particularly where Hutterite ministers are tempted to think they are having serious and meaningful conversations. While this medium can be effective for communicating trivial information such as the time and location of a meeting, it is far from ideal for conducting authentic conversations about real issues. In order to develop their ability as conversationalists, Hutterite leaders need a forum to regularly meet face-to-face to discuss relevant topics.

Preparing these presentations was an enriching experience in itself, as volunteers met to plan and discuss their learning and find a way to effectively share it with community members. By attending and responding to the different presentations, members practised and improved their communication skills and became more connected with people they had never had a deep conversation with before.[43] The outcome of these meetings was not a finely tuned policy regulating the use of digital devices, but a way to remind everybody that technology use has an enormous influence on our personal and social health, and that everybody has a responsibility to use it wisely. It is also worth mentioning that this process requires considerable patience and forbearance, and will be more difficult for people who are introverts by nature or may not particularly enjoy discussing a topic at length.

To return to the January 2018 Schmiedeleut Group I Conference meeting for a moment, there are several relevant points worth mentioning. Given the fact that dialogue skills are developed over time and depend on mutual trust between participants, spending a couple of hours discussing a complex, controversial policy that had held sway in the church for over twenty-five years is insufficient. A more patient, structured approach would honour the questions and concerns on both sides of the issue and would allow the time necessary to carefully study the scriptures and the historical record in search of guidance and direction. Beginning this difficult conversation is certainly a courageous and necessary first step, but the conversation must continue beyond the preliminary stage if it is to bear the fruits of understanding and unity. Tasking groups of ministers to study particular issues and leading discernment on them is one way to encourage learning and engagement. Building

---

43 By way of background, it is important to say a bit more about our context in Silverwinds. From 2012–2014, interested adults—about 25 people from teenagers to young and middle-aged parents to seniors, both males and females—participated in a community book club led by the author. From 2015–2016, parents met on a weekly basis to view and discuss Dr. Gordon Neufeld's *The Power to Parent* series on child development and parenting. Most recently about a dozen members participated in a weekly Reading Circle during February and March 2020. I believe these experiences were formative in helping our members develop interest and engagement in a broader set of issues, as well as competency as thoughtful readers and conversationalists. Book clubs hold a lot of potential for stimulating thinking about important issues and for developing capacity for healthy conversation.

capacity for discussion among the ministers is also a crucial first step before they can have the confidence to lead similar discussions in their local congregations. One way to do this might be to organize a reading group where ministers can meet regularly to read and discuss literature relevant to their ministry.

Sharing Circles

Another practice that has the potential to elevate discussion and discernment in our communities is regular brotherhood or community-wide meetings. In most Hutterite communities, important day-to-day decisions are made by a council that consists of the minister(s), steward, farm manager, and in some cases, one or more witness brothers. The larger (male) brotherhood is consulted when large purchases and decisions are considered, church discipline is enforced, and important public announcements such as baptisms and marriages are communicated. Theoretically, members have the opportunity to ask questions and provide insights that aid the discerning process when matters are brought before the brotherhood. In practice, however, the culture of decision-making in many Hutterite communities does not invite much critique, discussion, and participation.[44]

Over the last several decades, many Manitoba Hutterite communities have transitioned from a predominantly agrarian economy to one where industry represents a significant source of income. Formerly members worked in relative isolation for most of the day in the various barns and shops on the *Hof.* Manufacturing has afforded the possibility of the majority of the workforce working in close proximity. Together with the obvious need for regular communication between workers and the leadership team in a factory setting, these circumstances gave rise to a meeting I will call a sharing circle.[45] The male members of the community gather regularly,

---

44 For the perspective of an outsider who joined a Hutterite community for several years see Robert Rhodes, *Nightwatch: An Inquiry Into Solitude: Alone on the Prairie with the Hutterites* (Intercourse: Good Books, 2009).

45 A growing number of communities have circle meetings in one form or another. Some meet on a weekly basis while others meet daily. There are, of course, many different ways to organize a meeting. The benefits of the circle format are that it emphasizes equality, which invites participants to lower their defences and be vulnerable. Seated in a circle, members can make eye contact and the audio is opti-

typically once a week, to provide an update on the various work departments and to discuss issues that pertain to the larger community. Paul J. Wollmann has called it a "venting meeting" because it provides opportunities for members to express their concerns and grievances in a healthy manner. "Somebody who vents publicly can be helped," he observed. Overall, he thinks the sharing circle is an important forum "to iron out issues, allowing us to work peacefully in the workplace and in the larger community."[46] Further, he believes that the meeting space is a training ground that has improved Silverwinds' decision-making process by acting as a mechanism that keeps both the members and the leaders better informed about the needs and challenges the community is facing and thus more responsive and accountable to each other.[47] Zacharias Hofer, the facilitator of Silverwinds' weekly meetings, sees them as crucial for building a culture of openness and trust in the community.[48]

In the sharing circle setting, members become aware of what is going on in the wider community and develop the essential communication skills of listening, asking good questions, responding clearly and respectfully to questions, contributing expertise, and being involved in decision-making, all of which are essential for effective participation in the life of the community. In the close to twenty years that Silverwinds has practised this type of meeting, I have noticed how underdeveloped basic discussion and communication skills were for many community members, and also how they have improved with practice. In many communities there is a serious lack of communication and participation between the leadership team and the wider membership. Even within the management council itself there can be serious communication problems, leading to unsound financial investments and unresolved conflict.[49] Sharing circles are also a way to bridge the education div-

mal, approximating the ideal of face-to-face conversation. The circle also symbolizes unity and inclusion.

46 Jesse Hofer, interview with Paul J. Wollmann, July 2010.

47 When members are not informed of the financial circumstances of their community, they cannot help to address the causes of the financial problems by spending less, being more frugal, lowering the standard of living, developing stronger work ethic, travelling less, etc.

48 Jesse Hofer, interview with Zacharias Hofer Sr., August 24, 2019.

49 Interview with a member of Silverwinds' community council, July 2010. Asked whether the lack of communication between management and the wider mem-

ide. Teachers and older students—whose work in the school can easily isolate them from the community's adult population—have the opportunity to learn about what is happening in the rest of the community. In turn, other members get a weekly update on what is happening in the school. Of course, the weekly conversations also allow the exchange of ideas on many other fronts.

For the full potential of sharing circles to be realized, they would have to be expanded in several directions. First, such meetings would need to move from their mostly workplace function to invite discernment on other moral issues affecting the community, such as how to minister effectively to our youth, how to engage positively with non-Hutterite neighbours, and how to reach out to serve the less fortunate in our world—concerns that are at the heart of the gospel and the church's mission. Second, the voices of both men and women should be invited and respected in such public forums. If we take the body metaphor for a healthy church community seriously, as the scriptures and our sermons clearly teach, then we should be prepared to empower brothers and sisters—who took the same baptismal vows of faithfulness and accountability— as moral agents in the communal decision-making process.[50] The discernment process will vary between communities, given their unique needs and contexts. It will also require a robust, courageous faith and vulnerability as members grow at different rates in maturity and understanding and learn to accept differences. Finally, sharing circles require competent, sensitive leadership and facilitation to function in an effective and healthy manner.[51]

---

bership was a key factor responsible for widespread financial problems among Hutterites, he responded: "There is no question that that is the case. What I hear [about communities' financial circumstances] at the accountants' advisory meetings confirms this."

50 Traditional Hutterite homily for Pentecost, "*Erste Pfingsten Rede* [First Pentecost Homily]." Demonstrating the participation of God the Father and God the Holy Spirit in the life of the community, the author invokes Paul's instructions to the Corinthians in 1 Cor 12:11, 28. In the former reference, the Holy Spirit is said to direct the diversity of gifts in the community, while the latter reference describes how God ordained an order of offices that serve the community: apostles, prophets, and teachers, as well as diverse gifts and forms that work together to build up the church community.

51 Significantly, Hutterites traditionally called their ministers "servants of the Word" (*Diener des Worts*) and their financial stewards "servants of material needs" (*Diener der Notdurft* or *Haushalter*). This Christian servanthood terminology has to a large

Conversation and Daily Council Meetings (*Rot*)

Besides public meetings at the community level, there are many other opportunities to develop our capacity for conversation and connection in smaller settings. One such forum is the daily *Rot,* or council meeting, which is tasked with day-to-day planning, coordinating members' travel plans, and processing inquiries, complaints, and requests. The daily council meeting was first implemented in 1973 as a means to encourage closer collaboration between the secretary-treasurer, the farm manager, and the minister.[52]

A common understanding of what happens at these daily council meetings is that members ask for permission from the community council to travel somewhere or to follow a certain course of action. In that understanding, leaders wield ultimate, unquestioned authority, and members are discouraged from engaging in an open dialogue or offering any opposition to the decisions of their leaders. Understandably, individuals who hold this understanding often find it intimidating to approach the council. Further, many council members have been socialized to understand their leadership role in this way, which makes it a difficult dynamic to address. One problematic consequence of this approach is that members commonly rely on their leaders to make difficult decisions for them instead of discerning on their own whether a certain course of action is beneficial for the whole community. In effect, it is a way for members to avoid the responsibility to be directly involved in their community's decision-making and in the process to develop their voice, their conscience, and their ability to discern.

An alternative and arguably healthier approach is to understand the leadership team as a body nominated by the members to repre-

---

extent been replaced by worldly business terms such as "boss" or "management," reflecting a troubling trend of acculturation. The shift in language may also be related to our legal structure, where typically the minister is the president of the corporation, the steward the vice-president, and so on. Words are not neutral or arbitrary; changes in the language we use to describe our world are usually accompanied by changes in our thinking about the things we are describing, and finally, about how we live.

52 *Ordnungen und Conferens Brief* [*sic*] [Ordinances and Conference Reports] (n.p., n.d.), 70. See also Yossi Katz and John Lehr, *Inside the Ark: The Hutterites in Canada and the United States* (Regina: Canadian Plains Research Center, 2012), 297.

sent the interests of the community and give advice[53] to members with the big picture in view. For example, if I share my travel plans with the council, car-pooling with others can be coordinated. With this approach I am not asking for permission to do something, but sharing my plan or request and inviting the community's leaders to help me fit my plans into the rhythm of the larger community. In other words, when we come to *Rot*, we are participating in a conversation among brothers and sisters about our plans and the community's larger needs and goals. Understood in this way, community leaders are wise, patient conversation partners and not authoritarian gatekeepers who say "yes" or "no" without giving any justification or engaging in any kind of brotherly discourse. This understanding respects the individual integrity and dignity of each member and is consistent with the meaning of believer's baptism: it assumes that all brothers and sisters in the community are responsible and accountable decision-makers who are being formed as disciples through their participation in the life of the community.

At Silverwinds the council's meeting space includes an empty chair, which invites members to sit down and engage in a longer conversation with the council members if necessary.[54] This simple accommodation sends a powerful signal: that dialogue is a strength, an essential feature of a flourishing community. It is a reminder that leaders are there to serve and listen to their people, and they can do this best when people have the space, invitation, and freedom to speak their minds.

Conclusion

The Schmiedeleut church division of 1992 and the economic difficulties many communities face have brought to the surface a number of serious underlying conflicts and issues, including the underdeveloped capacity for communication among leaders and within Hutterite communities. Unfortunately, the skills necessary for healing any conflict—patient, charitable listening and open, honest speaking—have been largely absent and will need to be cul-

---

53 The *Hutterisch* term, *Rot*, comes from the German *Rat*, which means "council," and can also mean "advice" or "counsel."

54 Jesse Hofer, interview with Silverwinds council member, Zacharias Hofer Sr., August 24, 2019.

tivated to make progress in finding reconciliation and preventing similar schisms from happening in the future. Moreover, one of the marks of a healthy church is its ability to dialogue in order to foster unity, to work for reconciliation, and to exercise moral discernment. There are a number of serious issues and questions that all Christian congregations need to address through tough, vulnerable conversations if they want their communities to flourish. At the same time, communities need guidance and resources (possibly in the form of regular, albeit repurposed, *Gemeindeordnungen*) from the church conference level that can foster unity and encourage moral formation. It is encouraging that the current elder is speaking clearly to ministers about their responsibilities to lead their people in conversations, not least with respect to issues relating to the church division. At the same time, church leaders will need to be aware that leadership skills, especially the ability to facilitate a healthy discussion, are developed over time and will require much practice, patience, and perseverance.

Further Reading

John F. Alexander, *Being Church: Reflections on How to Live as the People of God* (Eugene: Cascade Books, 2012).

Dietrich Bonhoeffer, *Life Together* (Minneapolis: Fortress Press, 2015).

Alan Kreider, *The Patient Ferment of the Early Church: The Improbable Rise of Christianity in the Roman Empire* (Grand Rapids: Baker Academic, 2016).

Gerhard Lohfink, *Jesus and Community* (Philadelphia: Fortress Press, 1982).

Charles E. Moore (ed.), *Called to Community: The Life Jesus Wants for His People*, 2nd ed. (Walden: Plough Publishing, 2024).

C. Arnold Snyder, *Following in the Footsteps of Christ: The Anabaptist Tradition* (Maryknoll: Orbis Books, 2004).

About Jacob D. Maendel
(1911–1972)

Jacob D. Maendel was a Hutterite teacher, pastor, and community leader. Born in 1911 at Rosedale Community near Alexandria, South Dakota, he migrated to Manitoba in 1918 when Hutterites fled political persecution because of their commitment to nonviolence. He was chosen as minister in 1949 at New Rosedale Community and went on to become widely regarded as a leader ahead of his time.

In an era when it was considered good economic sense to clear wooded land for use as fertile farmland, he insisted that strips of forest be conserved as ecological buffer zones. Both the task of selecting the site for a new community and the work of establishing Fairholme Community (1957–1959) were informed by his deep appreciation for nature: Jacob insisted on an acreage of bush above the Assiniboine River, and ensured that the natural environment remains as intact as possible, thereby gaining a reputation as "a staunch defender of trees."

Jacob Maendel also had an ecumenical vision. Although Hutterites of the mid-20th-century were characterized by exclusivism and sectarianism, Jacob was open to learning from non-Hutterites in a way that was enriching for the larger Hutterian Community. His outward-looking vision of faithful Christian discipleship led to newcomers—families as well as single adults—visiting New Rosedale: some stayed briefly, while others became permanent members.

Despite his basic grade seven education, he was a self-educated life-long learner who read widely and introduced his students to great thinkers like Dietrich Bonhoeffer, Sigmund Freud, Helen Keller, and John Milton. Maendel understood the value of a culturally sensitive education and his vision led to the teaching career of Peter Maendel—the first Hutterite to attend and graduate from the Manitoba Teacher's College. This resulted in the unique dynasty of Maendel educators among Manitoba Hutterites today.

Ultimately, Jacob's vision and focus were the impetus for a surge of interest in education among Schmiedeleut I Hutterites that has culminated in nearly 100 Hutterite teachers holding Arts and Education degrees and teaching Hutterite children in their respective communities.

Jacob Maendel died in 1972. With gratitude to God for his work, witness, and inspiration, we name this lecture series in his honour.

About Jesse Hofer

Jesse Hofer is an educator, translator, and historian who is a member of the Silverwinds Community near Sperling, Manitoba. For the past fifteen years, he has taught Grades 5-12 at Silverwinds School, as well as Hutterite history on the HBNIITV system. In recent years, Jesse has also taught Hutterite history to adult learners, both online and in-person. He teaches Sunday school to youth in his local community.

Jesse has authored several articles on Hutterite history and theology, most recently an essay on cultivating communal conversations published in *Navigating Tradition and Innovation*. He co-edited the sourcebook *For God's Truth: A Hutterite History Reader* (2024). Jesse is one of the founders and organizers of the JDM lecture series and he sits on the committee of the Hutterite Historical Archives.